CW00567004

Letter from the Editor

Hello and welcome to The Cosplay Journal, a new and exciting bookazine* for the UK, focusing on the Diversity and Craft of cosplay. We want to show that not only can anyone from any walk of life be involved in cosplay, but also that we are all capable of learning new skills, creating amazing things and bringing joy into our own and other people's lives through the art of costume making.

Back in the misty depths of 2017 an idea was brought to me, to put together a cosplay book focusing on the UK scene and the amazing craft that is going on here, but there is too much going on to cover in one book. Several other countries have already got their own cosplay magazines going, and I felt that it would be great to do this for the UK and so I put it forward that instead of a book we make a coffee table magazine, with a good grounding in the community to highlight the diversity, ability and creativity of the UK cosplay scene.

And that is what you have in your hand, the product of eight months' worth of hard work from our small but passionate team; I cannot thank them enough for giving their belief and love to The Journal. Every single member of the team is a cosplayer and they love what they do, each showing that love in their own unique way, with their own unique talents, and hard learnt skills that they want to pass on so that others might fall in love too – if they haven't already.

I very much hope you enjoy The Cosplay Journal and help us build it to be a great part of the UK, and possibly international cosplay scene.

Yours,

Holly Rose Swinyard
Editor

*I hate this word, honestly, who invented it?

Holly Rose Swinyard
Editor & Head Writer

Holly was once described as a 21st Century Marlene Dietrich, but if Dietrich were British and a cosplay geek. A cosplayer for over a decade, and now working as a fashion journalist, Holly was the obvious choice to spearhead this new magazine for the UK cosplay scene, hoping to inspire cosplayers old and new alike.

Twitter: @lilistprince
Instagram & Facebook: @lilprincecostumes

Isa Shaw-Abulafia
Writer

Isa is a cosplayer who focuses on armour and robot builds. A designer for theatre and film, working in a variety of creative roles ranging from set and costume design, to the design and fabrication of masks, armour and props, she is also an organiser for TFNation, where he is a cosplay contest judge and co-hosts the cosplay panel.

Instagram & Twitter: @EvilCleverDog

Alyson Leeds
Writer

Alyson is a writer, historian and artistic Jack-of-all-trades, currently living in Bath. She has been cosplaying for five years, and is best known for her portrayal of Batwoman. On occasion she is mistaken for a serious academic.

Instagram: @latincatcosplay

Megan "Megg" Amis
Head Photographer

Megg is a photographer based in Surrey. Their first convention was back in 2010 where a camera was always in hand, although only in recent years have they actively taken up photoshoots to capture cosplay in its best light.

Instagram: @MeggoPhoto
Twitter: @MegNotEgg

Sophia Haden
Writer

Sophia is a professional Make Up and SFX artist based in Bristol. She has been a cosplayer since 2014 although these days you'll normally find her making costume pieces for other cosplayers rather than donning the costumes herself. Find out more about her work and get in contact about your own creations via: www.sophiahadenmakeup.co.uk

Instagram: @sophiahmua.sfx

Luke Kerrigan
Writer

Luke is a performance cosplayer with over eight years of experience under his belt. Specialising in live in-character work and cosplay tutorial, he is a member of the YouTube creative group Bandursnatch Studios.

Instagram: @xanthcosplay
Facebook: @BandursnatchStudios
YouTube: Bandursnatch Studios

Ian Sharman
Editor In Chief & Head Designer

Ian is an award winning comic book writer, inker, letterer and editor and also a voice actor and audio producer. He had an idea to do a book about cosplay and the sense to ask Holly and Megg to make The Cosplay Journal so much more than that. He's a little short for a Stormtrooper.

Twitter: @idsharman
Instagram: @iandsharman
Facebook: @iansharmanwriter

Jennifer Drewett
Writer

Jennifer is a twenty-eight year old cosplayer based in South East England. By day she's a full time administrator for a medical company, by night she writes articles on films and cosplay and organises inclusive cosplay comic cons around the country with her partner.

Facebook & Instagram: @drewettcosplay
Twitter: @msjennybean89

Chris Brown
Designer

Chris, also known as Redwood Creations, is an illustrator, graphic artist and designer with several years of professional experience. He works in every medium you could require, having designed websites, logos, banners, magazines, posters, book covers etc.

Facebook & Instagram: @redwoodcreate
Facebook: @iansharmanwriter

THE COSPLAY JOURNAL

CONTENTS:

For Markosia Enterprises Ltd

Harry Markos
Publisher &
Managing Partner

GM Jordan
Special Projects
Co-Ordinator

Annika Eade
Media Manager

Meiron Jones
Marketing Director

Andy Briggs
Creative Consultant

Ian Sharman
Editor In Chief

The Art and Diversity of Cosplay

Disclaimer: A number of the costumes depicted in this book are based upon characters from motion pictures, television shows, video games and/or comic books. The use of these characters may be subject to legal protection based upon various copyright and trademark laws. All rights to the characters in this book which are either registered or otherwise claimed as trademarks are fully reserved by the various corporations who own these rights. Markosia Enterprises, Ltd, and the authors make no claim to any trademarked character whose costumed depiction appears in this book.

The Cosplay Journal: Vol 1 ™ & © 2018 Megan Amis, Ian Sharman, Holly Rose Swinyard & Markosia Enterprises, Ltd. All Rights Reserved. Reproduction of any part of this work by any means without the written permission of the publisher is expressly forbidden. Published by Markosia Enterprises, PO BOX 3477, Barnet, Hertfordshire, EN5 9HN. FIRST PRINTING, June 2018. Harry Markos, Director.

ISBN 978-1-911243-90-8

markosia.com
thecosplayjournal.com

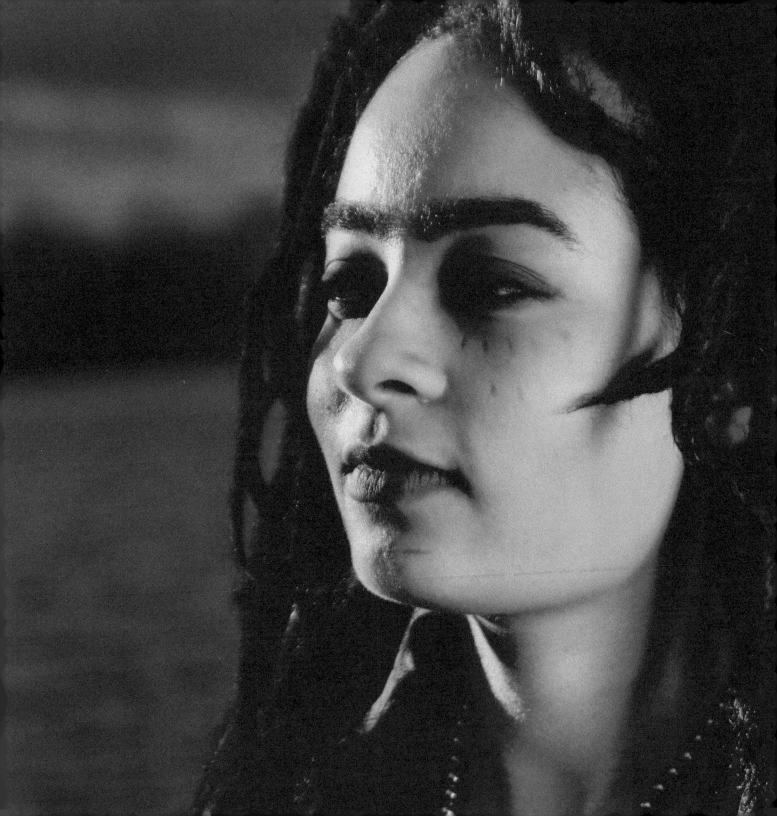

Emilia Harris: Tia Dalma - Pirates Of The Caribbean

The Cosplay Journal was lucky enough to shoot Emilia Harris, EmiliaDressesUp, in her incredible, period accurate, Tia Dalma costume from "Pirates of the Caribbean," and afterwards she talked us through how she went about making this eccentric costume and gave us a bit more of an insight into her work as a historical costume maker and why she loves this part of cosplay so much.

The Cosplay Journal: So, it's kind of mad, there is so much going on as a costume. Do you want to just start at the beginning, talk us through why you chose the character and how you went about building it, especially the more intricate parts?

Emilia Harris: I love Pirates of the Caribbean, I love pirates in general, I think they are really cool, and Tia Dalma is such a strong character. And also she's black so it's like, of course I have to do this! [laughs] I have to represent. It's really nice to see someone like that on screen, a powerful woman who's not there as a romantic love interest, she's there to play a major role in the plot, I really loved her. It was a bit of challenge making the costume.

I'm a costume maker by trade, but I started this, I think it was second year? Yeah, my second year of my costume degree, so I referenced things like historical fashion and costume. I checked the dates of when *Pirates of the Caribbean* was supposed to be set, so I looked at patterns in reference to that and it makes a lot more sense when you look at it as a historical outfit rather than a costume piece. So you realise she's actually wearing everything backwards; like she's got her petticoats and she's actually got her stays over her petticoats which is completely wrong and her dress is actually that [lifts the "coat" type piece of the costume] which she never wears, it's always sort of open and left out. I did that type of research which, overall, made it a lot easier.

TCJ: And you made all of it, even the stays?

EH: Yeah, I got the historical pattern online, because these are strapless stays. I ended up finding a pattern purely because I wasn't sure if they had strapless stays in that period, but it turns out they did, so that actually made it easier and I just made sure that I put all the sewing lines that I wanted on the stays themselves. If you look at the skirts and all the petticoats, those are tie on ones, so I *tried* to be as historically accurate as I could because I felt that was important. [Lifts up skirt] These are curtains though actually! [laughs] I was really lucky, managing to find a lot of stuff in charity shops and scrap schemes, basically I managed to get a lot of it for free, hunting around, the net and the trim as well were from there. The under skirt is the only fabric I bought new I think, you can see that it looks really lovely at the top still, above the weathering. You can still find this in Goldhawk Road, and it's so nice but I've absolutely ruined it for this costume [laughs again].

The one thing I didn't make though was this, the pendant. For ages I kept trying to work out how I would do it and I'm not a sculpting person, I can't really do that sort of stuff so I bought the official replica.

Her fabrics are quite specific looking but it wasn't as hard as I thought it was going to be, I was quite lucky with finding things that were as close as I could get.

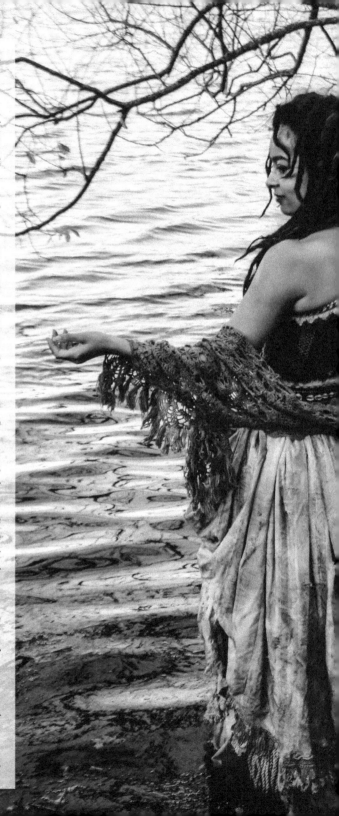

TCJ: It can be quite hard with film fabric, often they've made it especially for that costume or it's incredibly specialist, is it a struggle to match fabric for cosplays?

EH: Yeah, it can be, especially if the film is made in America or somewhere, you get completely different things over there. You'd think that by now everything would be everywhere but it is still quite different what's available in different countries.

TCJ: I love the belt, that's gorgeous! It's quite a different piece to the rest of the costume, how did you go about making it?

EH: I spent some time working that out, I wasn't sure if she had feathers on it but then I realised it was actually fur! I got a piece of, I'm trying to remember, it was a piece of leather I think and wrapped it around some buckram, and got *loads* of beads and threaded them all on. The shells on it, my mum had these for ages! She lived in Africa before I was born so I had loads of shell beads. I just ran home and was like "MUM! Where are the shell beads?! The time has come!" [laughs]. That was really nice; I enjoyed making it like that.

TCJ: There are loads of layers to this costume, it must have been a task to go about seeing what was going on, how many layers are there here?

Oh yeah! There's a few, the skirt is two but then there's like this fake layer with all the tassels and stuff on it, so I've just put another bit in there. I've cut bits off of other fabrics and stitched them on in random places to make it look more complex and have more depth. It's not as much as it looks. I just started breaking the costume down, piece by piece, to see how it all worked and I'll probably keep doing that as long as I wear it. I'm always going to be like, "It needs more, it needs more!"

TCJ: One of the things we really love about this costume is the weathering, it looks so grimy, which you really want for this costume, was that hard to do, ruining the costume you'd just sewn?

I cheese grated and sanded a lot of it down, and, yeah, weathering can be a bit scary, this was at first but it's such a big project that you just jump right in. It starts to look better the more you do it and that's when it's nice, but it's scary that first bit when it's like pristine. And that was quite nice because sometimes I can be quite, possibly

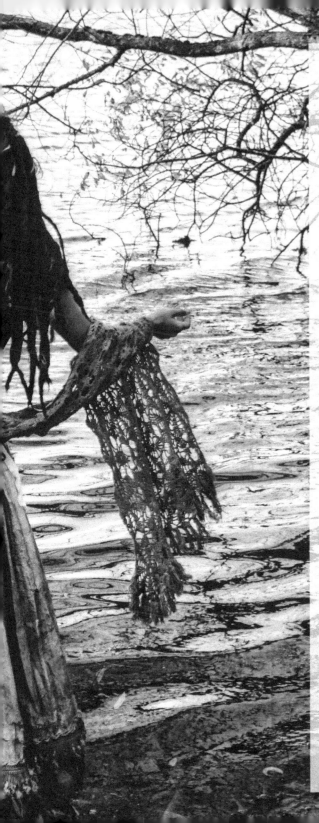

too, precise; it was just like, "You know what, this doesn't matter because I'm just going to sand paper this!" It was quite freeing rather than tricky.

TCJ: The wig is pretty amazing, it looks like real hair, what did you do to achieve this look?

I dreaded it, it's really effective. There are some great YouTube tutorials on how to do those, and it was so quick! It was pretty incredible. Because this costume is so messy I don't really have to worry about the wig, the worse it gets the better it looks! I added in loads more wefts to get a bit more colour in there and you just sort of roll it and back comb it, then use a wet cloth and steam the wig with it. It stays and it's magic! I did one and it was like, "Oh god!" Plus she has like feathers and bits sticking out of her hair so I could just put them in randomly.

TCJ: Is there any particular part of the costume that you are most pleased with?

Ooh, that's a tough one. Probably…oh I don't know. The belt I really like, and the stays, though I realised that I did the diagonal strips the *wrong way round*. They should go up the other way and I will be kicking myself about that forever! But apart from that I really like them. It works really well because it just gives you the right shape and you can tell that with a modern corset shape you get too much of like a dip at the waist, but these give the shape that's much more correct for the time. It really makes it look right and it feels right as well when you wear it which is nice. It's such good fun to wear; I feel really piratey [laughs].

With period pieces, getting the shape and the silhouette right is the most important part of it really, that's also why I did the double skirts layers because I knew that if I just did a fake under layer it wouldn't have enough of the volume and she has quite a voluminous skirt, so you need that extra fabric in it. Sometimes if you use a hoop it doesn't quite give the right shape but the underskirts do. This is so thick it pushes the skirt out just right, that was really helpful.

TCJ: Did you use any historical techniques in the build or try to emulate any in a modern fashion?

It was more emulating them. I probably would have used more historical methods if there had been anything more intricate or

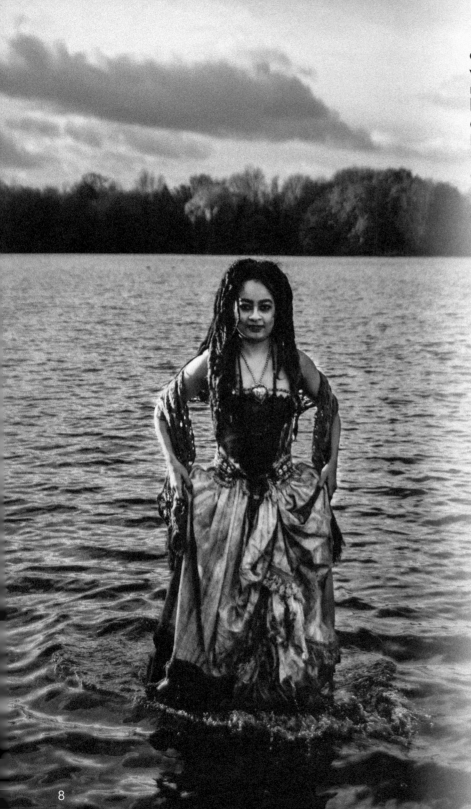

detailed on it but for most of it I got away with doing machine stitching, which was nice! I think some of the trim, I put on by hand [checks the stitching, laughing] yeah, definitely! It seems so long ago now, oh gosh. But I'm actually still quite happy with it which is amazing because normally you look back at things from about three years ago and go, "Oh god what is that?!"

TCJ: You do quite a lot of historical costumes, you've done West World and Black Sails as well recently, and you can completely inhabit these beautiful, historical characters, what is it about the period stuff that you prefer over things like science fiction?

That's a good question. Hmm, I think because of what I do, as a job, I like historical things anyway, so it does appeal in that way. Oh no, now I'm self-analysing. I think it's because I love things where people are being free, especially if they have maybe broken free. I love Vikings, I love pirates, I love cowboys, everyone is just going out and being free, having a good time, and I love the characters that are in those sorts of worlds, and I guess those worlds are normally period-centric, so I guess that's where it links up. I've realised that I stick with characters as well. Like I cosplay Missandei from "Game of Thrones" and I've done, like, five versions of her! It's the same with Max from "Black Sails," I just want to keep doing different outfits. I want them all. Maybe that's something to do with it too [laughs].

TCJ: There is often a feeling that you have to make a new costume for a convention and it can become very stressful, so do you think it's a better way to make costumes slowly and carefully, rather than rushing?

It's interesting isn't it? It's almost like a red carpet, you feel you have to wear something new every time and you really don't have to. If something's good it's worth wearing again and it's a shame. Sometimes if I make something I feel like I can't wear it again, but of course I can! I don't think there's any point in rushing. Obviously sometimes you *can* get things done quickly if you give yourself a deadline but I think rushing to the point where you're not happy with it is never a good idea. And if you can't produce something you're happy with then just let it go and you can go to the convention and have a nice time anyway. There's no point in stressing yourself out over it.

I mean it's nice when you and your friends make plans and then, you know, you've got a reason and you're pumped to do something new, but to push yourself to do it every time, it's a lot of work, and if you are really putting everything into it there's a lot to do. Most people it's not their main job or anything so to put that much time and pressure in, it's not good. I mean the London MCM Comic Con just gone, I did Missandei, but I'd started a new job the week before. Somehow I thought, "This is ok, I can do this in the week," and I don't know how I did it! I would just get home and it would literally be, "I have two hours I have to do this, this, this, this AND this." Somehow it all worked out and I was happy with it, but I couldn't do it again. I come home now and there's no way I could make a costume! If I'd had any more to do on that costume, if it were more complex, I would have just stopped, and called it on that con. It just would have been too much.

TCJ: Is there any advice you want to give to someone who is maybe starting out in

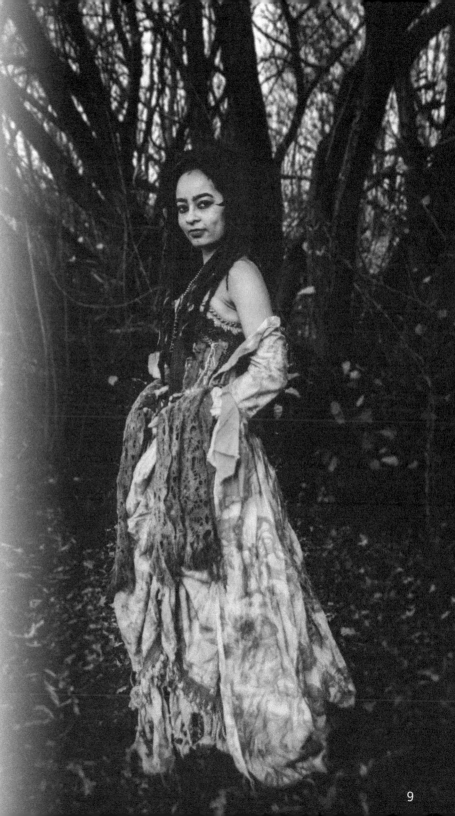

cosplay and looking at making costumes like this?

You just take it one bit at a time. Obviously something like this, when you look at it, even now when I look at it...just, "Oh my god this is a lot," but if you just take your time you'll be okay. That's what I love, that's why I do things when it's like five years gone because I look at it, then I go away, I think about it and maybe a few months later I look at it again, and then you might see something online and it clicks in your head. It's like, "AH! That's how you do it!" You just go piece by piece, don't let it all wash over you because next thing you're just piled under with loads of fabric, literally. Go slow and you will be ok in the end.

If you want to see more of Emilia's work and follow her up and coming projects you can follow her online:

Facebook: @emeliadressesup
Instagram: @emiliatarggaryen_

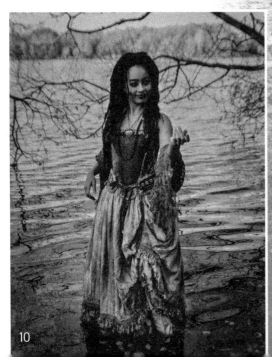

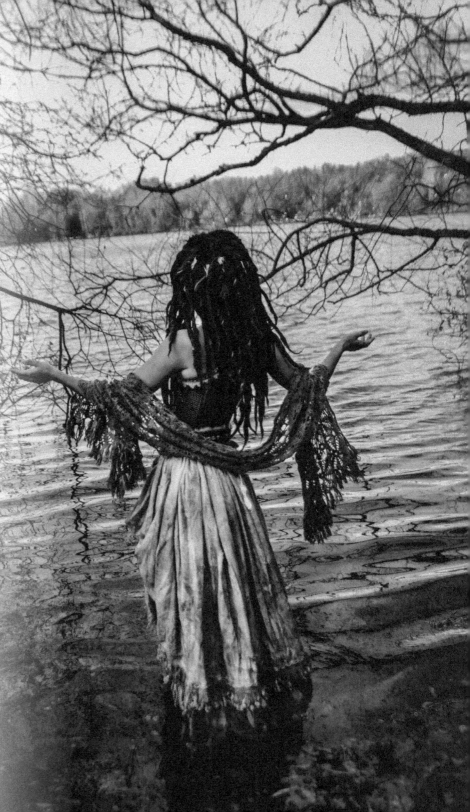

Editorial: My Life As A Cosplayer

Editor of The Cosplay Journal, Holly Rose Swinyard, gives us a look into their life as a cosplayer, and watching the changing nature of cosplay over the last ten years.

I have been cosplaying for over a decade, sewing and making my own costumes for the last seven years. I've learned and improved a lot since I started out, finding my feet and discovering who I am as a person through the adventures that cosplay has taken me on. There is more to cosplay than simply dressing up, as a community and as a personal experience, the world of cosplay is a place where many people have found strength and belonging. I've realised that my journey and progress as a cosplayer has shaped my life, taught me some hard life lessons, but also shown me how amazing and wonderful people are.

When I first started cosplaying it was a hobby that was planting its roots in the UK. Many people were already involved, and had been for some time, but it was really starting to flourish and grow in the early-mid 2000s. The manga publisher, Tokyo Pop, had started running small local events in book shops and were encouraging people to dress up and cosplay. For me, this was the first experience I'd had of cosplayers and I was completely hooked. At that first, tiny event not only did I

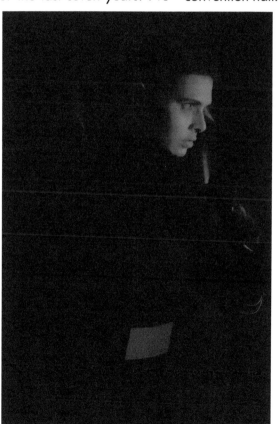

fall in love with cosplay but I made friends who became friends for life.

Those early days for me were full of the joy of learning to create and a desire to be like the veteran cosplayers that inspired me from the very moment I walked into the convention hall. It took me several years to really find my feet and to apply myself to learning to sew, but I always felt that urge to make and build, something I still have to this day. I feel that's part of why I have never fallen out of love with cosplay, because it gives me a purely creative outlet to improve myself, not just in my skill set but also as a person. I learned to be more open and supportive through cosplay, to share my ideas or my skills, to be someone who would help others and feel comfortable asking for help in return. I think cosplay made me a better person than I would have been without it. I think the community made me a better person.

That is one of the biggest factors in cosplay and one of the reasons that I think it has flourished as a hobby, the friendships and community that are built through it. There is a certain comradery in staying up until three in the morning helping finish each other's costumes the night before a convention. You don't forget the help that other cosplayers have given you, or you shouldn't at any rate. These moments make you stronger, more compassionate, more knowledgeable, all things that you can then share with the community as well.

As a hobby it has changed a lot from my teenage years as a new cosplayer, there is now so much more that you

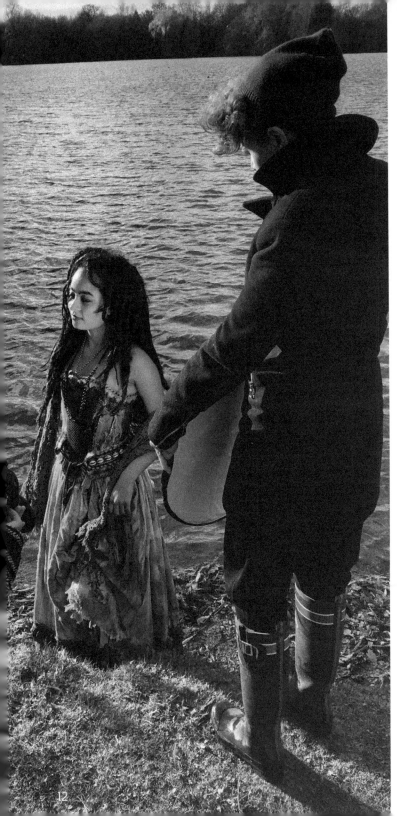

can access and get hold of to learn and work with than back then, that was only a pipe dream for my friends and I when we first started out. The internet has meant that we can now find tutorials of all shapes and sizes, styles and difficulties for every need and occasion; we have online shops selling specialist cosplay supplies at reasonable prices; there are literally ways of building costumes that didn't exist, or were incredibly expensive, that are now readily available at good prices. Thermoplastics, 3D printing, embroidery machines, printers that can print many different fabrics at a high quality, these are all becoming more and more accessible to hobbyists rather than being exclusively for professionals with large budgets, you can either buy your own or commission pieces online. The internet has opened up so many new ideas, materials and ways of working, and that's brilliant for the hobby.

The internet has also changed cosplay in other ways as well. Cosplay has become a lot more popular with more people getting involved every day, as well as non-cosplaying people becoming fans of cosplayers all over the world. It's spreading far and wide and people who would never have known about it before are now being introduced to it. This is obviously changing the nature of how we see cosplay. In some ways it's brilliant, opening up what has been a small hobby to larger audience is allowing people to become "cos-famous," giving the chance to make their hobby into their business, but this fame has also caused problems.

Our society as a whole is obsessed with celebrity, and it comes as no shock that there are those within cosplay who want that fame for themselves (or see cosplay as a short cut to fame with no real work). This is an incredibly small minority but to think that people don't see cosplay as skills and artistry that you love and have a passion for, but rather as means to an end possibly defeats the purpose of the hobby. This idea of celebrity culture can bring out a lot of negative feelings, causing people to think that they aren't good enough because they haven't got thousands of followers or enough likes on a picture. Much like the rest of society, there is pressure on

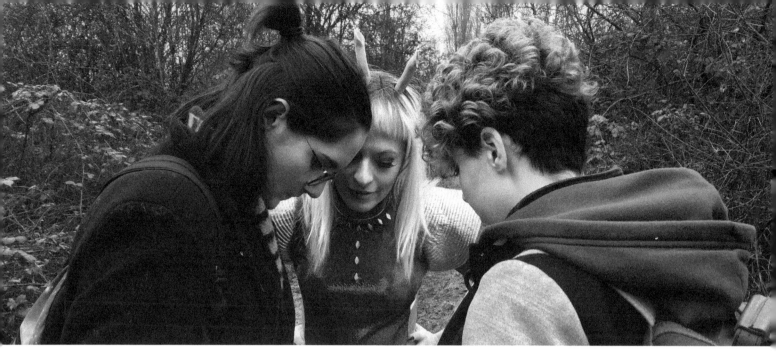

cosplayers to look and behave a certain way to please their "fans," but I fear with cosplay it is even worse than most hobbies, as this pressure is often astronomically high. Yes, cosplay is about appearance in some ways, you are dressing up as characters, but it should be about the appearance of the costume, the skill that you can see in its construction, the beautiful way it is put together, and the collaboration of creators in many different fields, not about whether the cosplayer is a size 0, what colour their skin is or if they are sexy enough for some random person on the other side of a screen.

However the opening up of cosplay is resulting in people building crazier and crazier things, looking to what is being made in America, Asia and Europe as inspiration and a drive to put the UK cosplay and convention scene on the map. We still lack the large competitions that are common in Europe, but each new convention season is seeing that change a little bit more, with more people wanting to compete at a higher standard and to take a place on the world stage. Not only that but I'd encourage more people to get involved in cosplay at a local level, having more and more cons appearing in towns and cities across the country, even just in village halls or sports centres, something that I feel is very singularly British in

its home grown nature and communal attitude. We're doing our own thing, while taking ideas and hints from the world outside. We're seeing what the international scene is doing and pushing ourselves to become better, not only as cosplayers, but hopefully as people.

The UK scene, unfortunately, does appear to have a reputation for suffering from a lot of "drama" that other communities do not, at least not at the same apparent level. This is something that has been a constant through my whole time as a cosplayer, and almost made me want to quit several times, but I, like many other, muddled through to find my own space that I could enjoy my passion in. It's a huge shame that our community is so riddled with the attitude that drama is part of what cosplay is, when that is so far from the truth. Of course there will always be some issues, but we seem to want to blow everything out of proportion, tell everyone what is going on and make mountains out of mole hills, I know I've been guilty of this myself in the past. There's no need for it. As my mother would say, "Don't hang your dirty laundry in public." Deal with it privately, there's no need to start witch hunts or spread gossip, come on, we aren't kids in the school playground.

All this being said there is a huge amount of good in the UK community. There are people doing everything they can to promote anti bullying campaigns, the community bands together behind campaigns such as "Cosplay is Is Not Consent" and to create safe spaces for cosplayers to talk and express themselves. Active efforts to get rid of the drama can be seen popping up all over the place, in smaller subgroups as well as the cosplay scene as a whole, building friendships and bridges in the UK and with international cosplay communities. After all, isn't that what all of this is for? To hang out with your mates and have a good old nerdy time? It's definitely what I came here to do.

Personally I think that cosplay will continue to grow and improve with each year that passes, and that will bring new challenges with it that we as a community must face. The changing nature of cosplay over the last ten years has meant that the community is bigger than ever, but there is still the feeling of everyone knowing everyone somewhere down the line. It's like a big family; it has problems and issues just like any but at the heart of it there is love and kinship for the hobby we are passionate about.

Holly Rose Swinyard

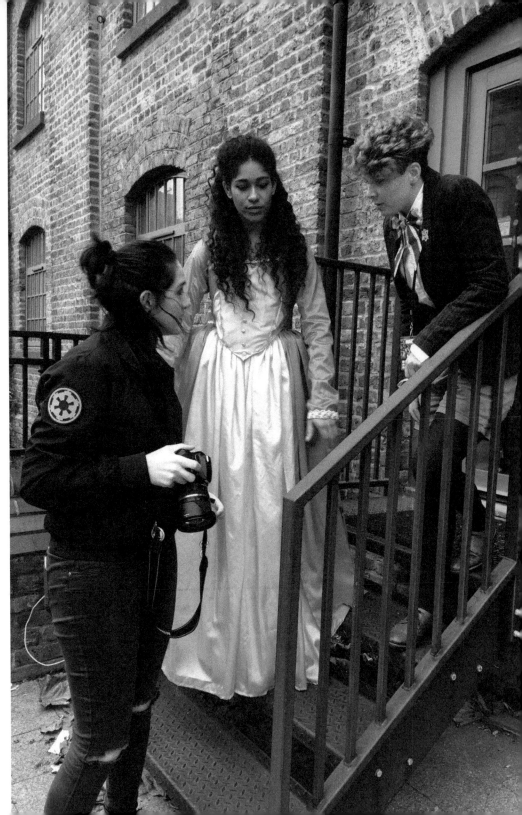

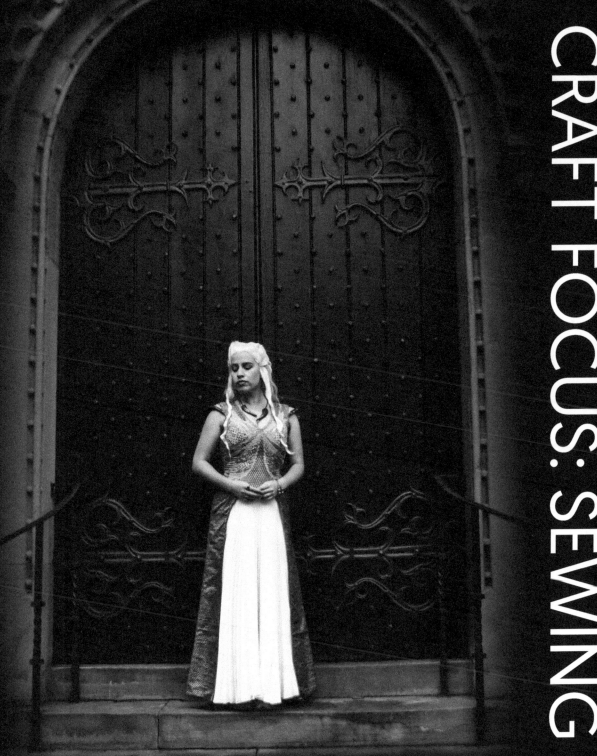

CRAFT FOCUS: SEWING

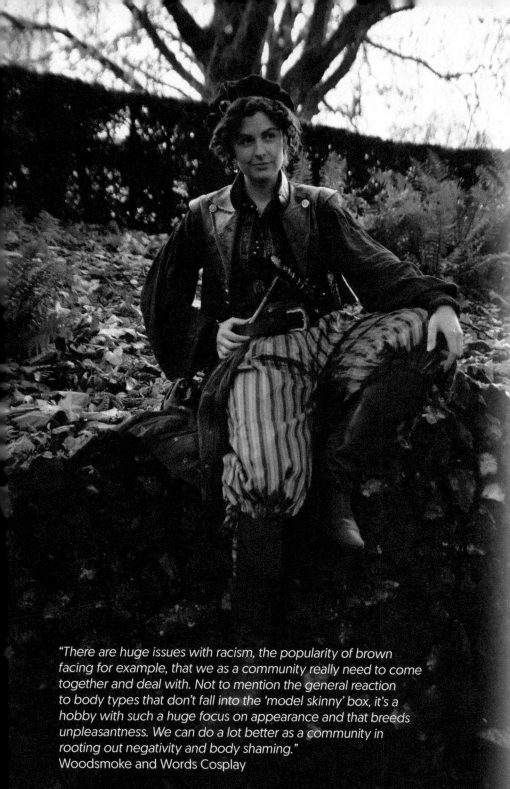

"There are huge issues with racism, the popularity of brown facing for example, that we as a community really need to come together and deal with. Not to mention the general reaction to body types that don't fall into the 'model skinny' box, it's a hobby with such a huge focus on appearance and that breeds unpleasantness. We can do a lot better as a community in rooting out negativity and body shaming."
Woodsmoke and Words Cosplay

Featured cosplayers:

Eleni - Chameleon Cosplay
Daenerys Targaryen - Game Of Thrones
Facebook & Instagram: @ChameleonCosplay

Tilda - Woodsmoke and Words Cosplay
Scanlan Shorthalt - Critical Role
Facebook & Instagram: @woodsmokeandwords

When you look at cosplay you are seeing the finished achievement of weeks, if not months, of hard work, often after years of learning the skills needed to create it. With each costume you see, that person will still be learning, improving and honing their craft the same as any artist does, hence why you have so many different mediums used to build costumes. The different elements of cosplay are vast and numerous, allowing for huge amounts of variation and individuality throughout the cosplay community. Individual cosplayers will each learn and master many skills, some will specialise and others will become more of a "jack of all trades" wanting to try some of everything.

There is no right or wrong way to cosplay or create your costumes, all the mediums that are used should be seen as equal and different. After all it would be wrong to judge a beautifully realistic landscape against a modernist sculpture; there are skills that a seamstress or a tailor may have that an armourer will not and vice versa. To truly appreciate cosplay you must understand each of these crafts in their own right and how often what looks simple has a lot more going on under the surface.

Fabric based costumes are one of the main elements of cosplay, using a variety of different techniques and skills to create everything from beautiful ball gowns to Jedi robes to military uniforms. Fabric can drape, stretch, gather, swing and fall in so many ways that you can do almost anything with it. There is a huge amount of variation with fabric, you can go from hard wearing leather that you need to punch through to stitch, all the way to silks and chiffon that flow like water but need to be handled with the utmost care. It can be both beautiful and practical; it's all to do with how you use it.

The thing with fabric that is different from other materials that you can use for cosplay, is that is it so malleable. No two fabrics quite work the same, even looking at basic cottons. You'll get thicker, heavier weaves and light weight, almost sheer ones, so knowing which one to use when and for what is crucial to making a perfect garment, after all not all your clothes are made from the same fabric. It would be boring if they were. With all the differences between fabrics, you can understand why they are such an interesting medium to work with. Simply cutting a piece of fabric in a different way to the last piece will give you a completely new thing to work with. You cut on the bias and you will get a drape or a waterfall type affect, cut with the grain and you get a strong, sturdy piece which, hopefully, doesn't warp. Just the simple thing of changing how you cut your fabric will change the

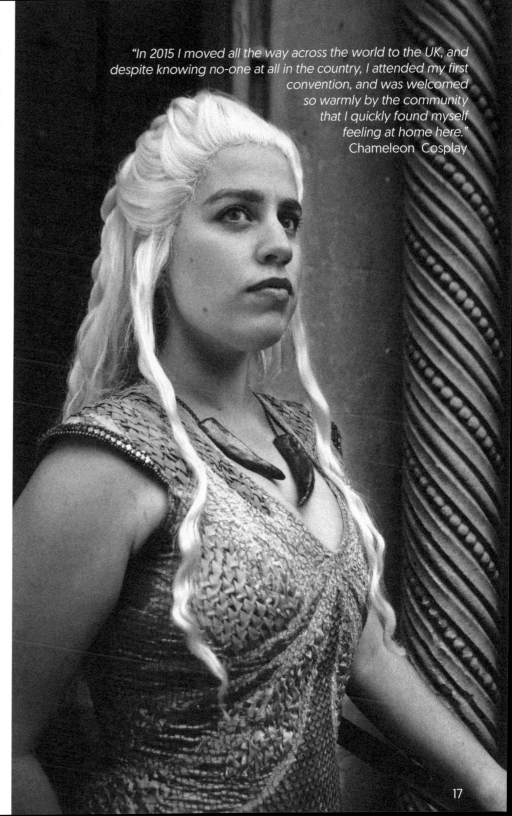

"In 2015 I moved all the way across the world to the UK, and despite knowing no-one at all in the country, I attended my first convention, and was welcomed so warmly by the community that I quickly found myself feeling at home here."
Chameleon Cosplay

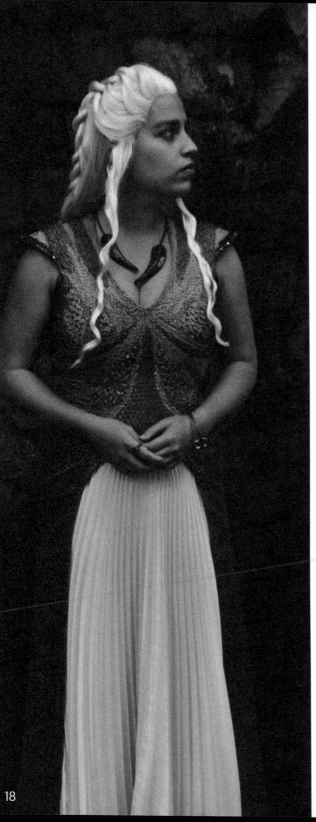

whole look of a garment and that's before you start even putting it together.

Changing the fabric you make a garment from changes the feel of the piece. You make a coat from a heavy wool, it will swing and hang, fall around the wearer like a protective barrier. It's practical, sensible in many ways, it speaks of someone who is prepared, but you make that same coat from silk and satin and you have a very different piece altogether. No longer a piece of practicality, now a statement of luxury and possible frivolity or wealth; it will flow and move with ease, delicately encasing the wearer and floating out around them. Clothing is the biggest visual indicator of personality that we can use and so for costume it is like a language to tell everyone looking at you what that character is like and how they behave. It also helps to dictate how the cosplayer should act when wearing it, how to stand, how to walk, it's amazing how much it changes how you feel when you put on a costume. When it comes to cosplay that choice of fabric is so important because it's going to reflect in all the other aspects of the costume and wearing it.

Of course fabric is not the only thing important to sewn costumes. Far from it, after all two metres of fabric does not a costume make. Putting garments together requires not only a degree of skill but also a rather large amount of patience, no matter what type of costume you're making.

There are many techniques that can be used in the creation of fabric based costumes, starting at basic levels of construction all the way through to pattern making and decorative techniques such as beading and embroidery. As pretty as embroidery is, it's worth taking a look at tailoring and dress making as they are the building blocks of any garment. Even if you are just starting your first piece you will be sewing fabric together into a shape and that means that you are learning these skills.

The difference between dress making and tailoring is something like the difference between cooking and baking. They can be seen as different things, though they carry a lot of the same skills and techniques.

Many people would say that tailoring is more about the fit, making sure that you get it perfect, so it is not strictly limited to "masculine" garments, as you will often need to fit a blouse or a pencil skirt. You want to be looking at the way you shape the garment right from the get go, making sure that the pattern is creating the fit and cut that you want, building a shape for the garment. Tailoring something means that you are looking at the garment as a whole shape that will sit in a certain way. But surely dressmaking is about that as well? Because fitting a bodice does not mean you are not thinking about the skirt, in fact the fit of the bodice dictates how the skirt will sit and fall so is that tailoring or dressmaking?

In all honesty the differences come down to what you like to make and what you like to practice. Personally I can whip up a pair of trousers and waistcoat in my sleep but the thought of a bodice scares me to death, even though I've made plenty in my time. If you can do one, with a little thought, you can do the other. At an amateur level, you are likely to be chopping and changing a lot, though I'm very sure that professional tailors and dressmakers would tell me that there are myriad differences between the two. For most cosplayers, this is not our jobs – though often people do go on to train – and so it is very helpful to be able to have skills across the board with sewing.

But trust me when I say that making a collar sit tight to the neck so that you can wear it properly is one of the greatest trials any one, no matter their technical leaning, will ever have to endure.

Beautifully sewn garments are fascinating to me. Seeing how each seam has been put in, how crisp the finish is and the perfect lines of the piece is one of life's

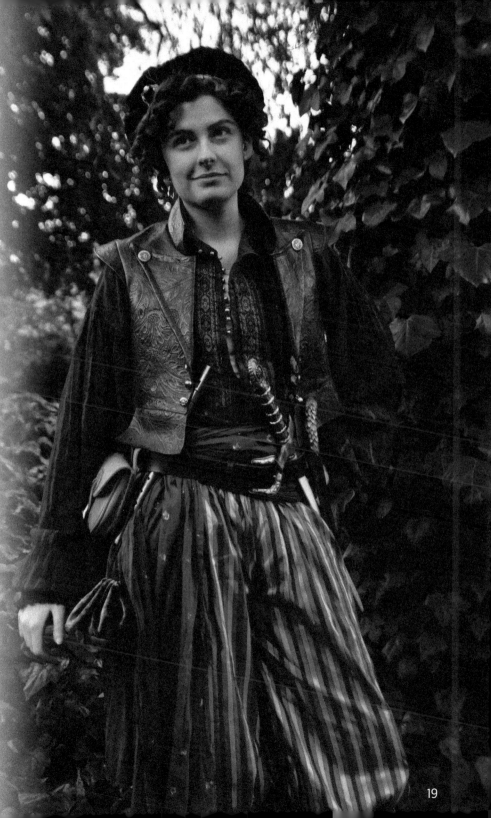

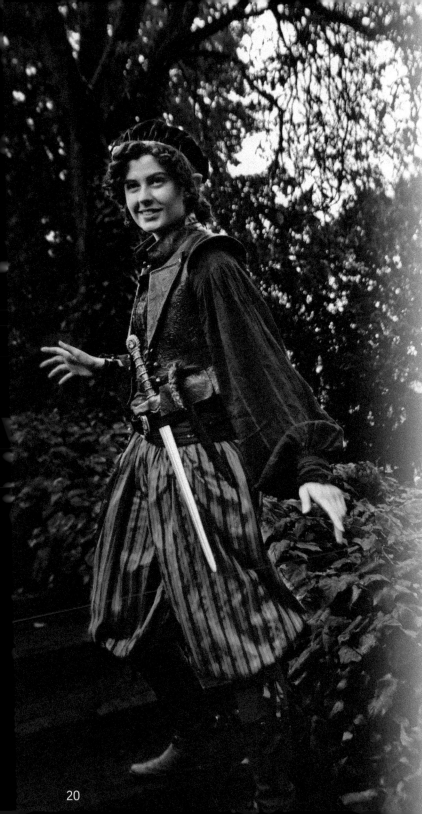

great pleasures, if you're me, but sometimes a costume needs more embellishment. It may be that the original design has patterns on it or it could be that you feel that it is too simple as just a piece of clothing.

Adding detail to a costume allows for it to have more depth. It stops being a "costume" and starts to look more like a real garment. If you look at a pair of trousers in a shop, they often have top stitching, embroidery, studs and patches on them, so costumes that really stand out reflect this idea of added detail, because it makes them more realistic. This can be as simple as some topstitching along the edges of seams, not only is this a practical addition (holding the seams flat) it adds a bit more texture, depth and realism, really finishing off a garment.

Embroidery is one of the best known ways to add to a costume. It's very obvious when you see it and stands out with the many stitches and thread types you can use to create elaborate designs and patterns on the fabric. Hand embroidering is one of the easiest things to start to learn. And I don't mean that it is easy to do, but it is easy to start and that's what matters. Learning a few basic stitches, like a blanket or chain stitch means that you can put a nice, but simple, edge on a garment (especially good for a "rustic" look) and you can build your skill set from there. This is the same with any embellishing technique, not always quick to learn but can soon add a whole lot to your costumes. It's all down to taste, some people will like a nice bit of crisp top stitching and not much else and others will want lace, embroidery, beading, gem stones, the whole thing. And it could just be that you want a fancier version of the costume or that might be what the costume looks like from the get go.

Everything about cosplay is personal preference and you can see that in the way that each cosplayer makes their costumes. It's not just about which characters they pick, it's also about their way of sewing and building a costume. For me this is what I love about sewing, that you can see how each person interprets something differently despite having the same references.

I see sewing as my way of expressing my love for characters, clothing styles and cosplay in general, and I know that I have my own unique way of doing that, as does every other cosplayer. I love making costumes look like they exist in the real world, picking fabrics that match the practicalities of the character, making them in ways that make them feel less of a costume and more like clothes. I want it too look like the characters I cosplay are as real possible, that's my way of cosplaying. Other cosplayers want to look like they've walked right out of the video game, comic, cartoon or whatever it is they are cosplaying from, and seeing how they achieve that look is just as cool. I love seeing how people recreate the same thing in a myriad of different ways; did they use silk brocade or layer patterned chiffon over satin? Is that canvas or cotton? Can you achieve the same fit with darts as you can with a corseted back? It's worth trying everything as it can all look amazing and I love that there is no wrong way to do anything.

I said that cosplayers are artists, and just like any artist, we have our mediums and our own stylistic choices that make each one of use unique. No two cosplayers are the same, no matter what.

Holly Rose Swinyard

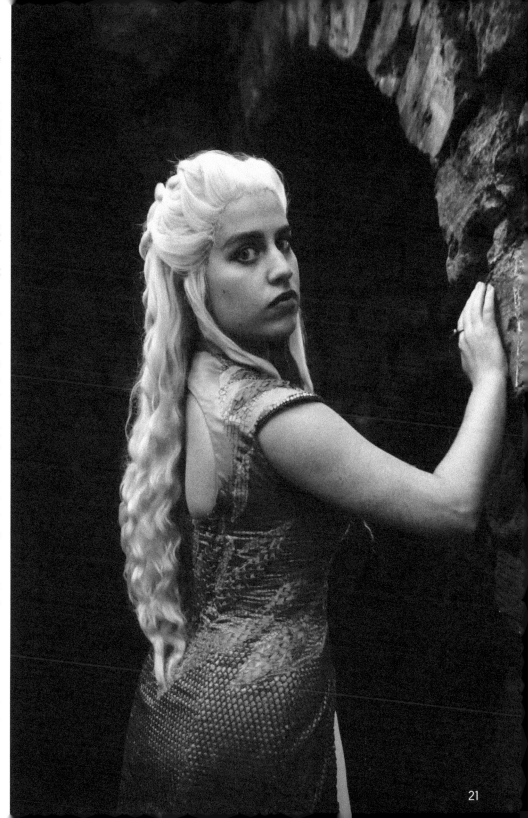

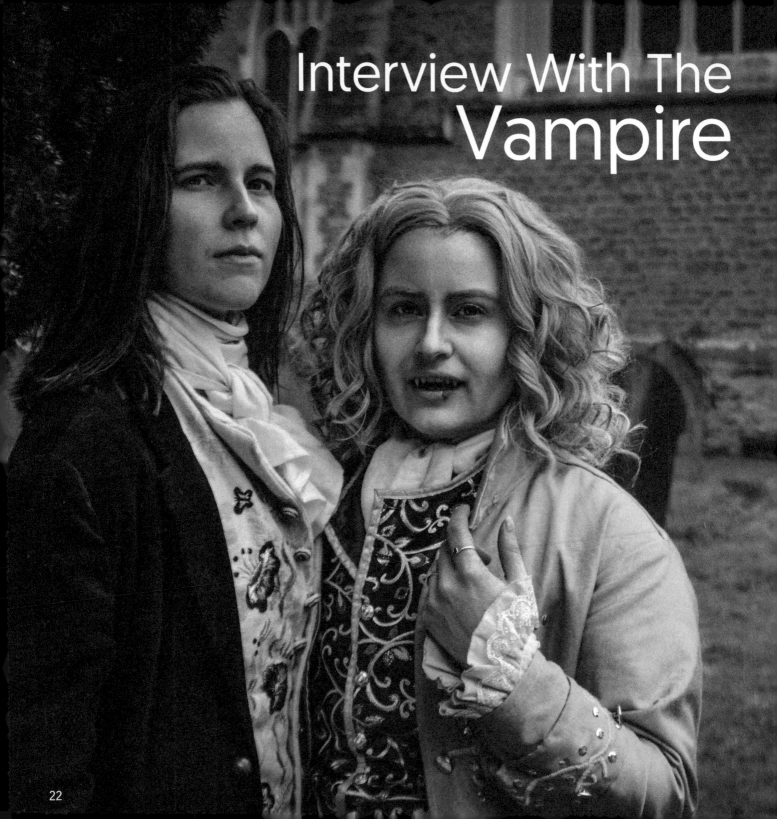

Interview With The
Vampire

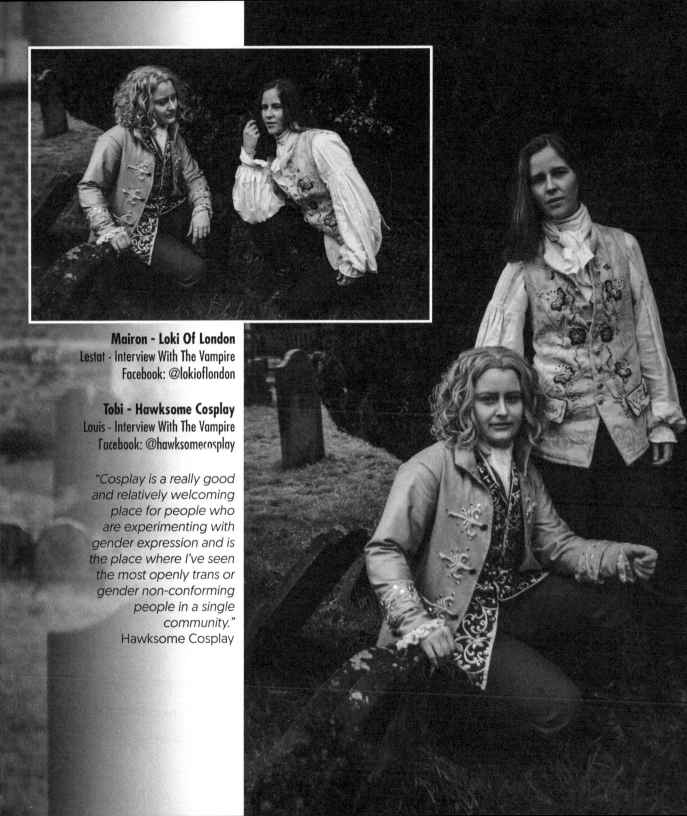

Mairon - Loki Of London
Lestat - Interview With The Vampire
Facebook: @lokioflondon

Tobi - Hawksome Cosplay
Louis - Interview With The Vampire
Facebook: @hawksomecosplay

"Cosplay is a really good and relatively welcoming place for people who are experimenting with gender expression and is the place where I've seen the most openly trans or gender non-conforming people in a single community."
Hawksome Cosplay

ZENIBA

"I think what I really like to do is to learn new skills! Cosplay is a constant learning experience for me. Obviously, sewing is my main skill and where I feel most comfortable; I still push myself with every outfit to try new things."
Weatherwax Cosplay

Kerry - Weatherwax Cosplay
Zeniba - Spirited Away
Facebook: @weatherwascosplay
Instagram: @stitchy_mcbitchy

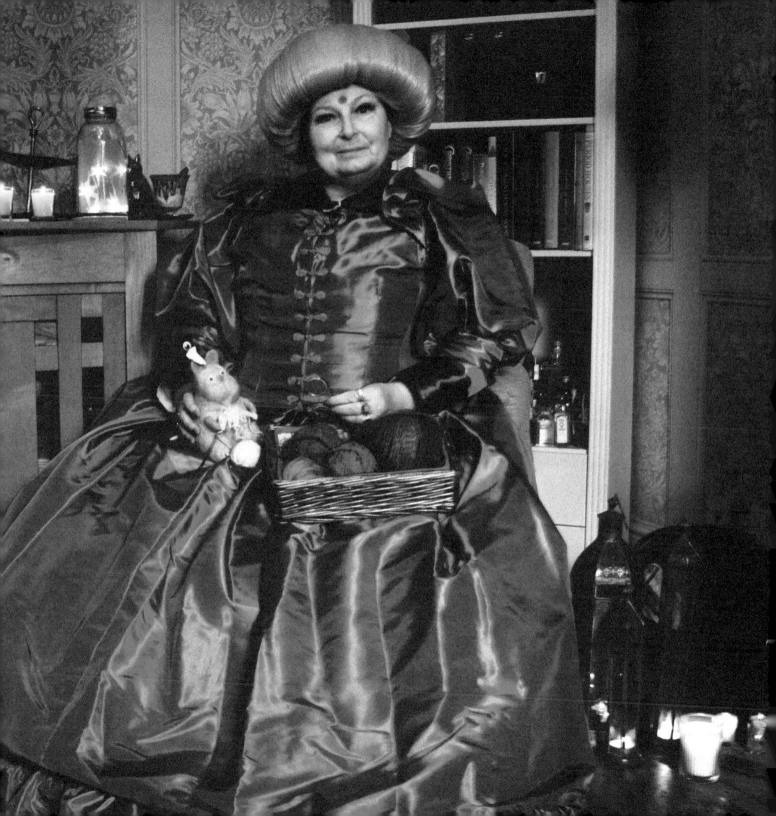

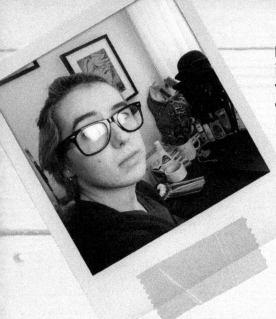

In our house weekends are cosplay days. Depending on the time of year these dedicated "cosplay days" might be mainly dedicated to meetings and emails with guest bookers and convention organisers, or as convention season kicks back off, the dreaded "Con Crunch." Regardless of time of year, though, Sundays are always livestream days. My partner and I are members of a larger cosplay performance group,

Bandursnatch Studios, who specialise in live panels at conventions and video content (be it tutorials or skits or crafting live streams) for YouTube. For us, and the rest of our group, this means that the "play" part of being a cosplayer is at the forefront. Most of us are from a theatre background of some description, and while the crafting and fabrication aspects of the hobby are important to us they can't possibly compete with the feeling of breathing life into a character and bouncing back and forth with audience members in a live setting. Existing in a bubble, without interaction with others, is a near impossible thing for a performance based cosplayer to do, I have found from experience, and these streams go a long way to making sure that we keep ourselves in top form, even during the quieter season. Few things are particularly constant in my life as a cosplayer, but; a loathing for sewing in sleeves, an impatience for glue drying and knowing that from 3pm to 6pm every Sunday there will always be at least two members of our team frantically glueing, sewing and, most importantly to me, interacting with the people watching the stream, are all guarantees. Nothing is worse than a rusty actor, I've found that

being able to regularly interact with the rest of the group, snap up questions and respond in interesting ways really keeps our gears oiled as a team.

But this isn't really telling you too much about an average Sunday in what we affectionately call "The Bandur Nest." Sadly our day doesn't start in a way that would be too dissimilar from anyone else's who works a full time job through the week, being a cosplayer unfortunately doesn't stop the bathroom from needing to be cleaned or the hall from needing vacuuming (sometimes it even increases the frequency

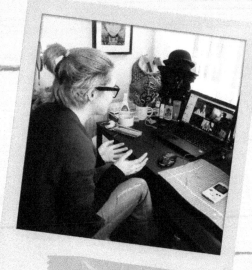

A Day in
the Life
of a...
COSPLAYER

these things need to be done). Flash forward to the fun part though, once we have thrown ourselves round Tesco, have it all away in the fridge and have made the second "last" trip out to Hobbycraft; it is somewhere between quarter and half past two which means it's time to set up the cameras and get everyone's microphones synced. Thankfully, this is not a job that falls to me, as our less than lightning fast internet a few years ago meant that we were unable to host the main call for the stream. Our preference at the moment is to stream from a group chat on Skype to YouTube, which works pretty well for allowing us to see and hear each other in real time with minimal delay while leaving us enough of a delay to YouTube's inbuilt text chat to be able to respond to our viewers in a timely manner. This pre-stream time lets us have some much needed quasi face-to-face time with each other as our group is made up of cosplayers from all corners of the UK.

Once it hits 3pm and our promo goes up on the Facebook page, then it's time to go live, and so begins three hours of vaguely controlled chaos. The thing about our craftstreams is that we have always been a little vague with defining the rules of exactly what we want them to be. They started out as a good way to make sure that it was easier for us to fill our two videos a week quota

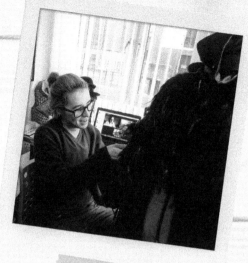

> *"...it's the chat that makes the livestreams what they are..."*

while everyone was working full time, while not having to sacrifice fabrication time so that we could record specialised content. This means that we can have days when there are all six of us furiously hot gluing and wig styling, and there are others when there's just one person crafting and someone else is solely attempting to shepherd the chat. Obviously, even cosplayers who have year-round commitments like us run out of content and projects to work on now and then, and there have definitely been Sundays where we have struggled a little to find things to fill our "creative allotment" for the weekend. I remember there had been a week on the run up to Christmas last year when my partner and I had been so overwhelmed with work deadlines as well as our festive recording projects that we ended up putting up our Christmas tree for the livestream…in partial cosplay. I will have to admit that this was probably the most we have ever phoned it in, so to speak, for a stream but it ended up being really good fun for us and the viewers. Live streams can be really good for humanising you for your audience, as there can be a tendency, I have found, especially when cosplaying through Youtube, for viewers to forget that it is just other people doing this for a hobby.

As I have said earlier, it's the chat that makes the livestreams what they are, the streams may give us content but it is the live chat with our blessedly ever growing viewers that really keeps us fuelled, and I like to think it's a mutual thing. It lets us field ideas that we want to try on the channel with our viewers and also lets them suggest to us what they would like to see more of from us. The big bonus of the craft stream though will always be that it makes us have to put everything else down and work on our projects. The idea of having a couple of hours of your weekend when you can just get down to doing some good old fashioned costume making with your friends and that not only can you share that experience, but also encourage people to take that time to do something constructive and creative, just really inspires me as a creator. Some of my favourite streams have had viewers crafting alongside us, sending in work in progress shots to our Facebook page and asking for help or ideas

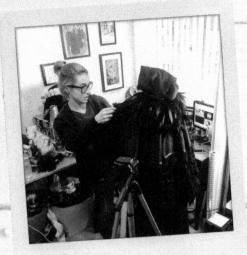

for how to complete certain parts of their costumes. This little feeling of community, cosplayers helping cosplayers and sharing their knowledge, or simply getting really excited over a fandom or an up and coming con is just incredibly heart-warming to experience. So often people talk online about how negative the cosplay scene can seem, so being able to be in a position where we are able to actively try and change just a small corner of that is very fulfilling.

Being able to allot time to "having" to work on my projects really helps me to guilt myself into working on projects that I am avoiding, especially if I say in the previous instalment that I am going to work on a particular thing. A little bit of positive pressure to please can go a really long way. There are always certain crafting activities we try and save for off camera. These are usually things which will either be very difficult to film or will possibly mess with the audio. We have since implemented a microphone mute rule to anyone who intends on using their sewing machine during the stream after the quite frankly ungodly noise someone caused once when trying to persuade their machine to go over three layers of leather. Heat guns have faced a similar run in with the "Ban Hammer" recently.

We usually run the streams for between two to three hours depending on everyone's life commitments that week, though our work doesn't stop when we go offline. Usually we have a little informal debrief after, which inadvertently ends up being an extended chat and continued private craft party, but then it's time for us to get back on track with what we jokingly call "having to adult." There is something comforting about working with a team of people who, even if we are all of varying ages and professions, understand the commitments that come from having to work a full time job alongside your passion. There is a feeling of camaraderie in having to put down the fun paint project to have to go make your lunches for the rest of the week, because as much as we live for our hobby, we also need to be able to finance it. I feel working with people who are in a similar boat to you and understand these silly little life struggles is part of what makes us such a strong group.

So the live stream is over. We've all muddled about avoiding having to hang up the washing in the machine long enough and it's time to go do that grown-up thing now, but what makes what we do so good is that it doesn't go on forever. It's a nice little break for everyone on a Sunday afternoon when you just need a little something to do, be it watching a couple of idiots try and power their way to a costume deadline or to try and hand sew on twenty one metres of feather trim onto a cloak. I like to think it has a little something for everyone. Trying to think about what your average cosplay day is like can be quite hard in a hobby that requires you to be constantly changing and evolving, but I think that's what makes this the perfect hobby for me.

Luke Kerrigan

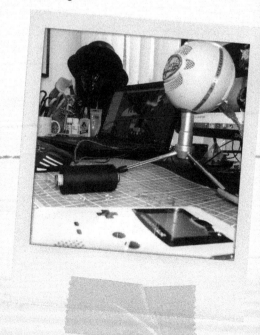

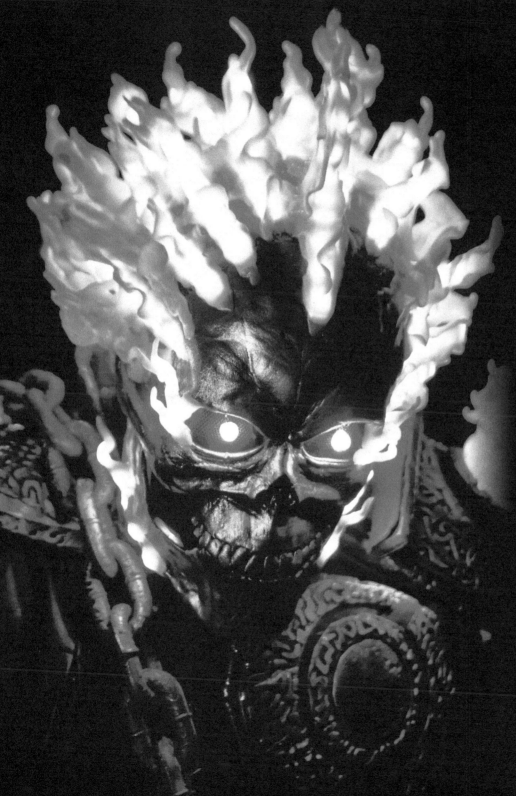

ELIJAH AKIBOYE
GHOST RIDER

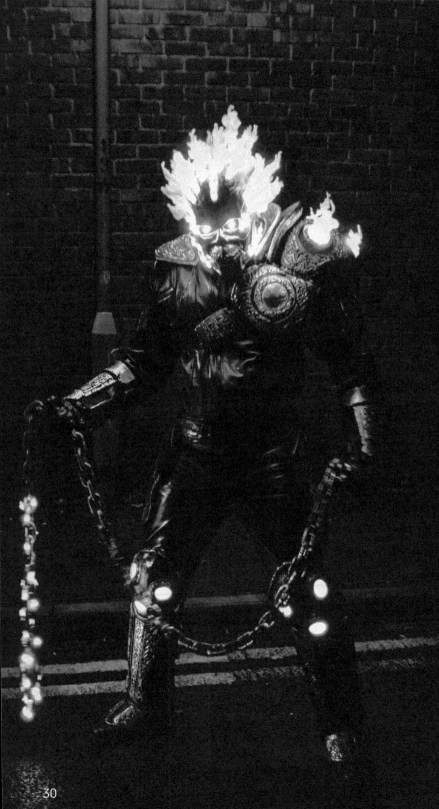

The cosplay world is full of amazing crafts people and Elijah Akiboye of BladesFortuna Arts and Cosplay has been pushing against the mold in the UK cosplay scene with his amazing creations for the last few years, working on new techniques and ideas to make each of his costumes bigger and better. With his most recent costume, Ghost Rider, he has, in our opinion, raised the bar in what can be achieved with thermoplastics and armour builds. Our editor, Holly Rose Swinyard, sat down for a chat with him about this incredibly challenging build and his time as a cosplayer.

Holly Rose Swinyard: The costume is amazing, you've actually talked a lot today about the build, while we were shooting, but unfortunately that wasn't on tape [laughs] so if you could tell us how you put the build together and what inspired you to do such an incredible looking character?

Elijah Akiboye: Obviously I'd made a couple of costumes in the past, and originally I'd had a plan that I was going to stick to and this year was going to be "the big cosplay" but in between finishing stuff I ended up going on Instagram and just seeing a couple of Ghost Rider costumes and got a bit side tracked. There was one really good one by a cosplayer in Australia who does some amazing stuff like Deadpool and Wolverine, and I'd really liked it. But I was looking at this costume, and it looked great, but it got me thinking why doesn't anyone try to actually do an illuminated version of the flames or anything like that, you know? Maybe just in sculpted form or something and I just said, "You know what, maybe I should give it a go." So I think around, say, December last year (2016) I started just looking for skulls online and then it went on to me not being able to find them and then saying, "Yep, I have to make this thing myself." January this year (2017) I managed to

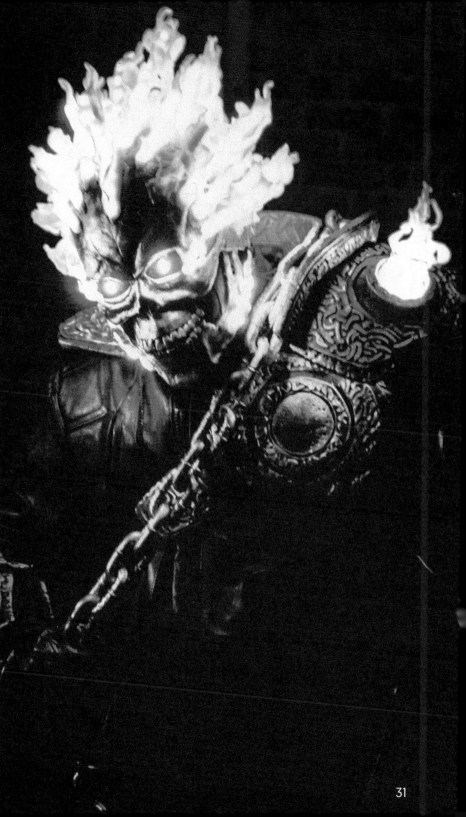

get, like, a top face skull mask which was solid enough for me to use thermoplastics on and ended up using it to make a full Worbla skull. From there I went on to research what kind of materials to use for the flames.

HRS: You used Polymorph plastic, which I hadn't heard off before today, and it looks so much more organic than any of other thermoplastics I've seen.

EA: It is, it is! Essentially it's these little pellets and what you do is you put them in a pot or a bowl or something and you can either use a heat gun to warm them up or you can use hot water, I generally use a heat gun just so I can control it better. Oh, it's very, very sticky! [laughs] So putting non-stick paper in the bowl is a must or you'll never be able to use it again. [laughs again] You can use your hands, very carefully, or with non-stick gloves because it gets really hot on your hands as well, to just shape it into any shape you want. It's kind of like clay or Plasticine, but when it sets it sets really, really hard. Not only that but the actual quality of the plastic is very flexible as well so you can't crack it, it's super flexible so you can bend it and it won't damage the shape. I just thought that would be an interesting material to make the fire out of. To be fair, between all the steps of actually making the head piece, obviously first making it out of Worbla, making sure it fit comfortably, making the jaw piece...

HRS: Oh, the jaw is separate isn't it?

EA: Yeah the jaw is separate coz it's the only way I can get my head into the skull without it all falling apart!

HRS: It honestly helps it look more realistic for me, having the blacked out sections, from the under mask, above the jaw, in the cheek area.

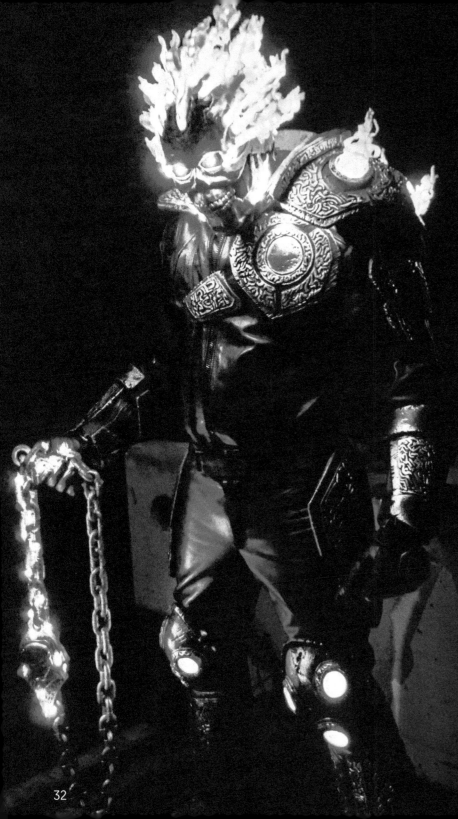

EA: And it's articulated from the actual piece itself and a lot of the time when you get these skull masks, they're made as one piece and then slit for a mouth as opposed to it being a completely separate part.

HRS: That's interesting because I did some work with a friend of mine who made the skull mask from the being from Spectre for a shoot and she'd done the same to make the jaw separate so you could get that more realistic feeling as well as talk and kind of drink [laughs]. It's very important.

EA: It's totally important! The funny thing is with this costume is that now it's all together I can't actually move my jaw up and down [laughs], because that's what I wanted when I was making the costume, that I could talk and eat, but it needs more than a single pivot articulation – oh that's a bit of a tongue twister – but, yeah, it's still the only way I can get the jaw on and get the head piece on in a way that will allow me to, you know, seal it in and walk around as the scary spectre of the Spirit of Vengeance.

HRS: What's the thing that you are most happy with, especially in such a complex build like this, there must have been something that you are really pleased worked out.

EA: One the things that I'm most impressed with is the fact that I was able to get the LEDs to work with the Polymorph plastic to get the fire effect. A lot of the time when people actually use materials for the flames or fire, they might use polythene or acetate and originally I was going to use acetate as well, but the problem with acetate is that if I was going to pack the costume away it would get crumpled and folded and I would have to spend God knows how long having to make sure that it was ok and sorting it all out; panicking the whole time. So making it out of polymorph, it did make the piece a bit heavier but at the same time it made it so much more durable as I can pack it inside a bag or a suitcase and not have to worry about it getting damaged. As soon as I fish it out I just have to go, "Ok, are the lights working?" and then it's good to go.

HRS: Your costume's a bit of a redesign, isn't it? Why did you decide to do that rather than working to other people's art?

EA: Yeah! It's my own rendition of the Danny Ketch character. I just thought it would be really cool for me to play around with it, coz I did the same with my Green Lantern and to a certain extent my Snake Eyes costume. I always like to put my own design spin on established characters just because it makes you more distinctive.

HRS: I completely agree and it's something that should be encouraged in cosplay. Do you think it adds to the creativity of the community?

EA: Oh yeah! It encourages creativity and individuality in costumes. The more people design their own stuff the more cosplayers will go into costume design, and many already do, and it'll be good for the community. It's great!

HRS: You've got the shoulder pauldron, why did you decide to go for that sort of element in the design?

EA: When I was coming up with designs for the costume, I was going online and looking at as many pictures as I could of the character, just to see what different artists had made him look like, and every artist had kind of the same thing. There were these spikes coming out of the shoulders, there were huge pauldrons on *both* shoulders, they had like the leather coat and they had the leg-grieves as well that had spikes in them and the glowing

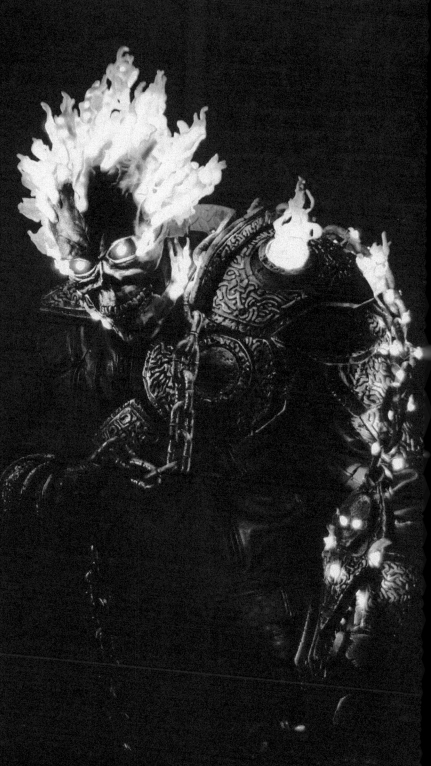

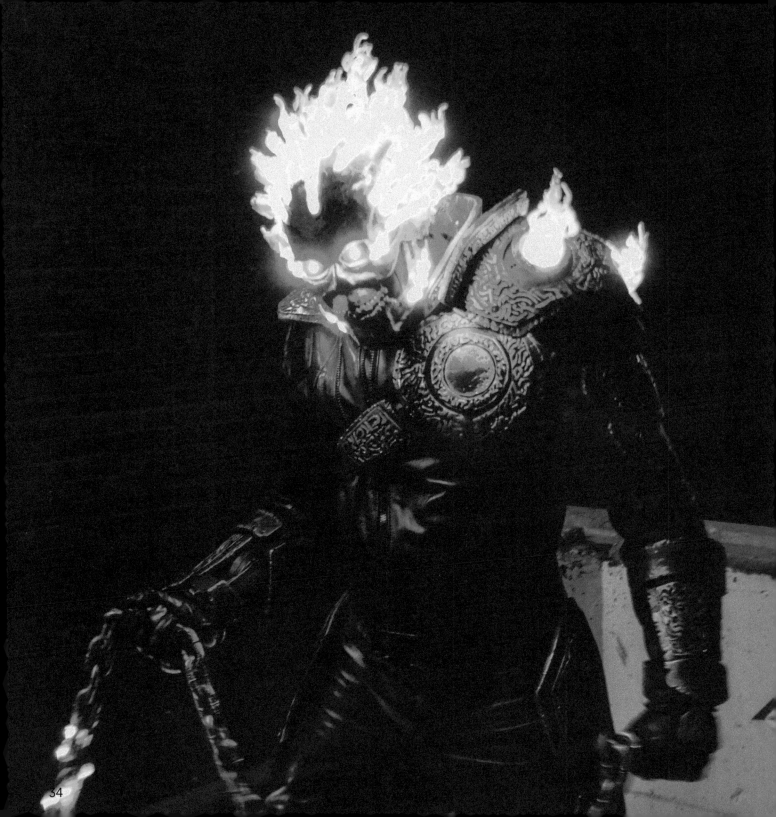

kneecaps. Then there was this particular piece that I saw that had this very, very paint-like equality and depth in how it was rendered. It was the cover of this comic that the blue Ghost Rider would be staring in, Danny Ketch Ghost Rider or something like that, and it was basically a picture of the character, standing with his chain with the spiked end, both spiked ends, standing in a very sort of manly way or something like that [pulls a face and laughs]. Anyway, it looked really, really good and even the skull was illustrated differently. It was completely blue, it was like *bathed* in flame rather than just coming off the top; it was completely engulfed but you could still see the skull underneath clearly. So that inspired the whole, "Let me try to make a little bit more of a medieval but kind of extravagant warrior spirit of vengeance," design. And the reason I went for the pauldron, the single pauldron, was because asymmetrical designs are a lot more, I think, appealing in terms of design instead of having two pauldrons. I think if I had gone for two pauldrons it probably still would have looked great, but I feel that, well one, it was less work to do [laughs] and secondly it just gives the costume a lot more dimension than if I *had* gone for two pauldrons. Some of the toughest characters in fiction wear pauldrons as well, so I figured him wearing one would be rough as hell – no pun intended – and the fact that he could slug it out with someone if he really needed to. Like I said, just the aesthetics of the design seemed to fit very appropriately with what I was going for.

HRS: The LEDs are great, there was something you said about the LEDs earlier, going into the polymorph that they worked well, did you find that you had any problems working with the electronics?

EA: So I had this happen when I first put the Polymorph onto the LEDs on the skull, I was pulling the LED strand and covering it with the Polymorph and I got to the third strand, I think, but the way I was pulling the LEDs on the head meant that the connections started to come loose. You've got to be careful when you're dealing with wiring in custom electronics, or any sort of electronics, simply because wires can come loose. On the rear base of the skull the join of the wires to the LEDs themselves were coming off the back! So when I was moving them around to try to get the best position to do the heat gunning and the forming and shaping, one of the LEDs

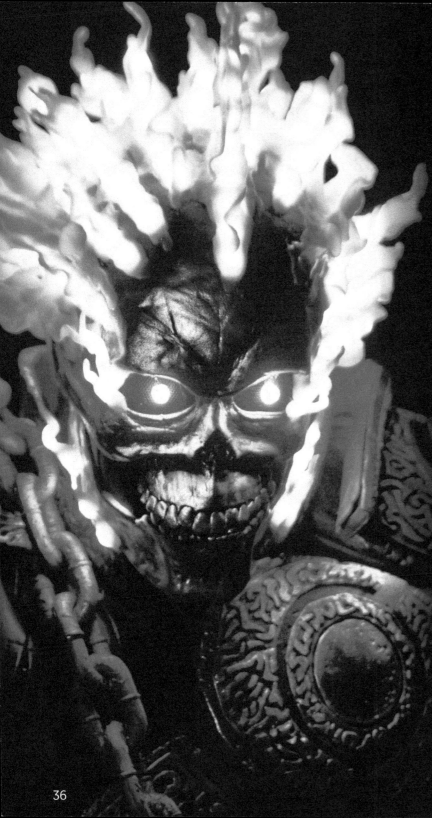

stopped working, because they'd been flexed too much. It was the most annoying thing. Looking back in retrospect, I probably could've only thrown the one LED strand away but I ended up just taking the whole thing off and, what made it even worse, I actually ripped them off the Worbla and took some of the paint off as well. So I had half this skull that had already been primed and painted in metallic blue and weathered as well, have this big black spot on the back where you could see the Worbla. It wasn't the worst thing in the world, because I could easily go back and re-prime and seal and redo it all again, but it was so easily avoided. Next time round I went for the mandate of, "I'm just going to put all the LEDs on, one by one, and then I'm going to do the Polymorph afterwards," and that ended up working out kind of beautifully but it just took a long time. Not only did I have to make sure that the Polymorph covered as many of the LEDs as I had, I had to also make sure that the sculpting and shaping looked kinetic enough and fluid enough to look like flame. The thing with Polymorph is that if you don't shape it properly it looks very lumpy and can look really disgusting and ugly, so when you turn the LEDs on you see the silhouette of the bumps in the glow. It could have looked more like a cloud head than a flame head. It took me a long time to tweak and make sure it looks right from each and every angle.

HRS: Would you say that making the mistakes helped you make a better costume in the end?

EA: I do think so, yes. On a basic level I'm surprised that the project went as well as it did. I thought there were going to be all sorts of other problems, maybe the LEDs melting or not working because they were subjected to too much heat when I was doing the heat gunning or something else like that. The little speed bumps I ran into, in way, helped me realise what I could do differently if I ever approached this project or a similar one again. All the problems I ran into did help me out in the long run and they helped me make something that hopefully will last a long while. Obviously the products I used were expensive but they'll last longer and will mean I can keep wearing it. Lots of things were considered to make sure it went as well as possible, the wiring in the eyes and making sure they were covered so you couldn't see any of that or my eyes, and all the electrics with the flames and keeping it all hidden and attached, it was all worked out.

HRS: Am I right in thinking that you're completely self-taught?

EA: Yeah, yeah I am. I like looking at tutorials on YouTube and the like for tips and tricks but not outright direct "one to one" sort of following along, more just to get an idea of how something works or how to put a certain thing together. I think it's a good way to learn and improve, taking the ideas and tailoring them to your own project.

HRS: Over all are you happy with how it came out?

EA: Oh yeah! I'm pretty damn happy with it, even the stuff that went wrong. [laugh]

To see what else Elijah is doing check out his work on:

Facebook: @bladefortunasmatrix

Instagram: @bfortunas

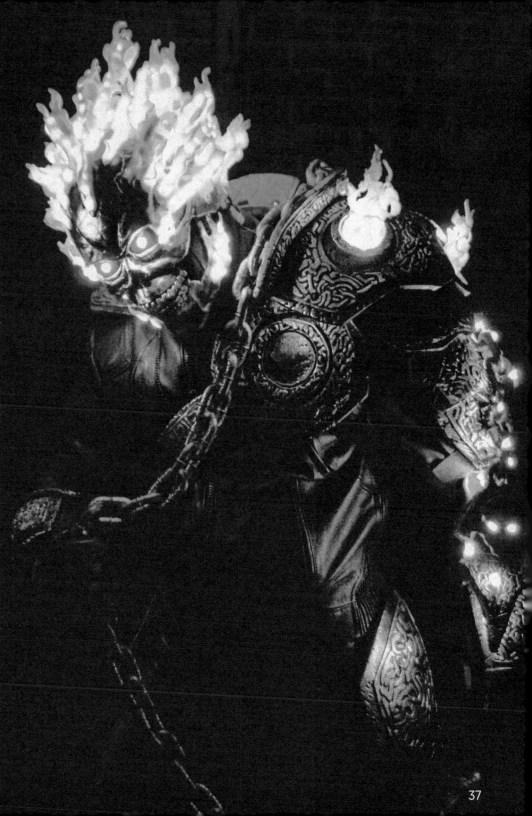

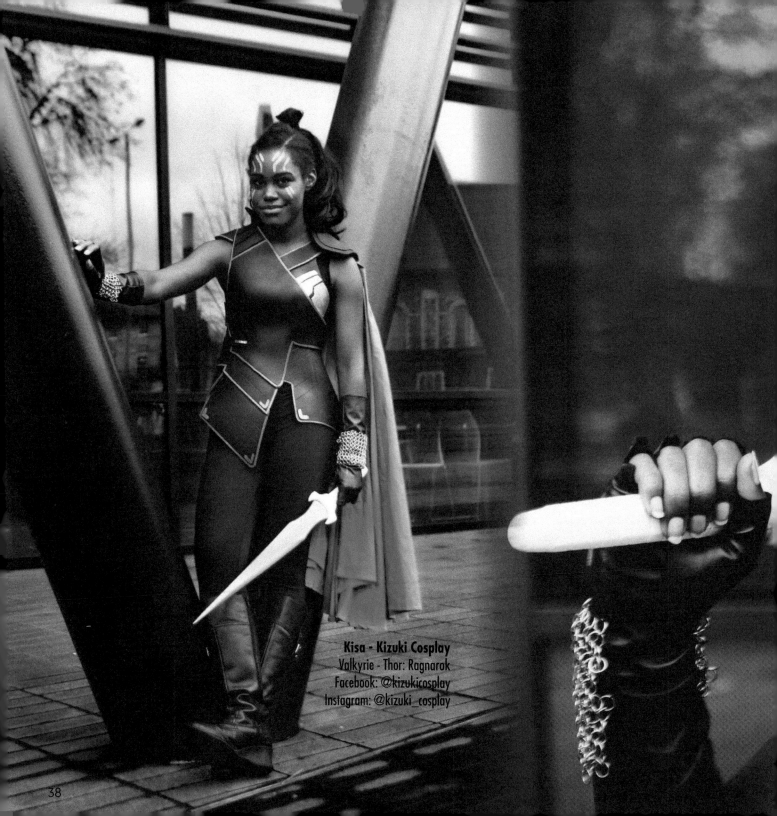

Kisa - Kizuki Cosplay
Valkyrie - Thor: Ragnarok
Facebook: @kizukicosplay
Instagram: @kizuki_cosplay

Valkyrie

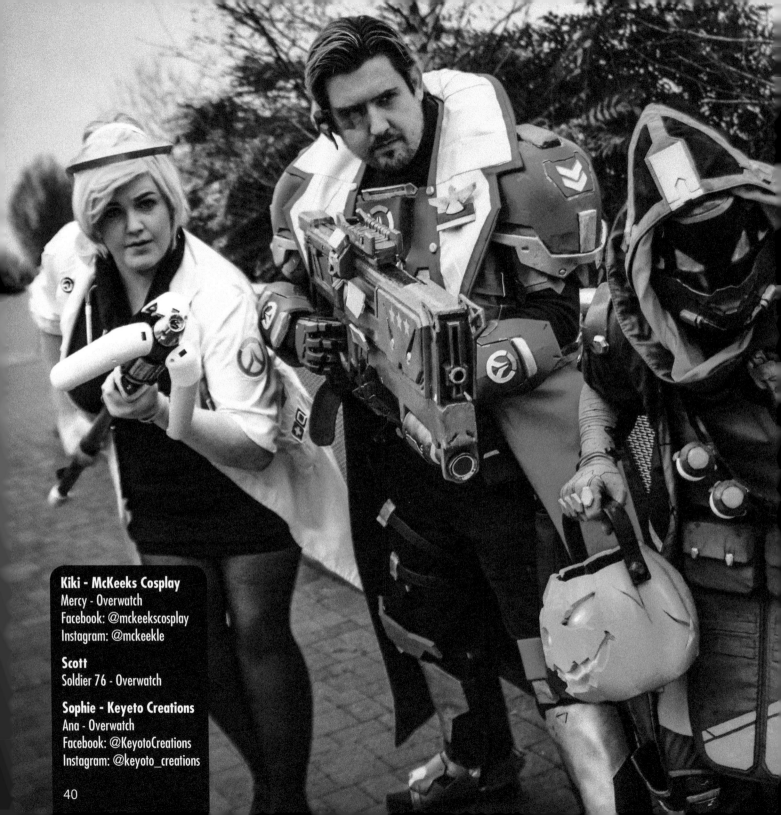

Kiki - McKeeks Cosplay
Mercy - Overwatch
Facebook: @mckeekscosplay
Instagram: @mckeekle

Scott
Soldier 76 - Overwatch

Sophie - Keyeto Creations
Ana - Overwatch
Facebook: @KeyotoCreations
Instagram: @keyoto_creations

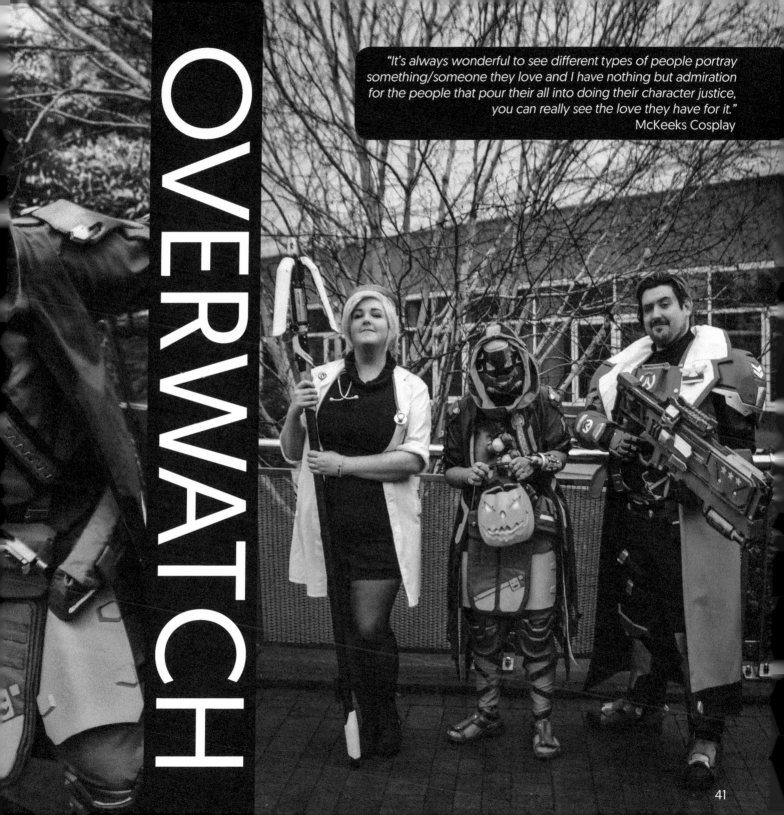

OVERWATCH

"It's always wonderful to see different types of people portray something/someone they love and I have nothing but admiration for the people that pour their all into doing their character justice, you can really see the love they have for it."
McKeeks Cosplay

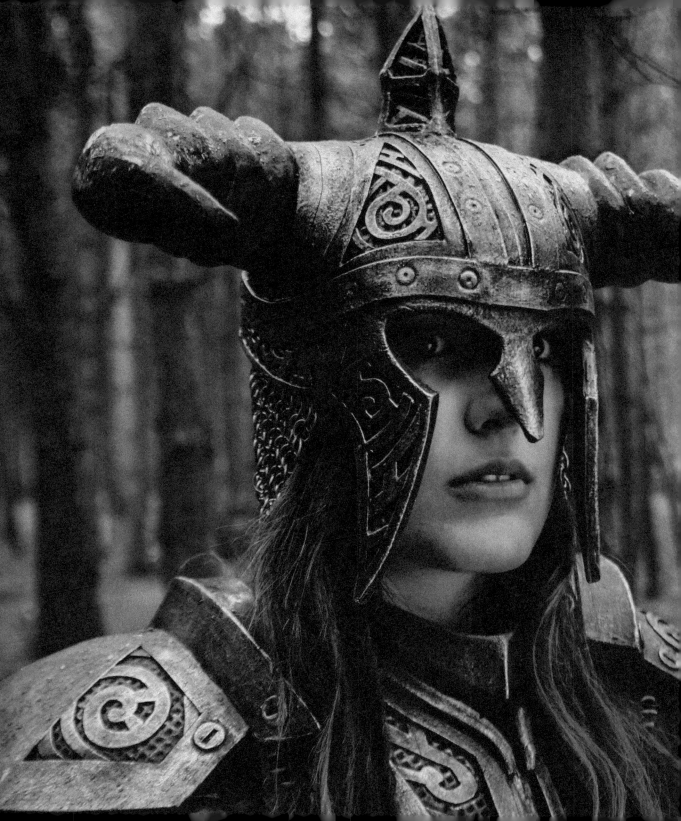

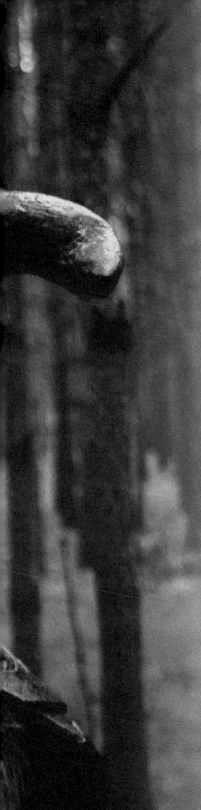

Making foam armour is an incredibly creative process, and I personally liken it to sculpting. This, as someone with a theatrical design and fine art background, is perhaps one of the main reasons I found myself falling in love with making costume armour so quickly. The creative problem solving involved with drafting, fabricating and painting foam armour is something that I find incredibly fulfilling as a designer, a maker and an artist. Making armour for cosplay has been a fantastic way to explore and experiment with these interconnecting disciplines.

When it comes to why I choose to cosplay armour specifically above other kinds of costumes, the visual appeal of robots and armour, alongside my enjoyment of the making process, is absolutely a factor. There's nothing more badass than a cool suit of armour or a giant mech, and what is cosplay for if not getting to feel like a total badass sometimes? I've also long been fascinated by armour, both as cultural artefacts and as practical, protective garments. Not to mention my interest from a design point of view, which now spills over into the ways in which armour is designed and used in fictional settings.

In terms of costuming techniques, armour sits in an odd place somewhere between costumes and props. Many of the same materials and fabrication techniques cross over between armour and prop making, as they do between armour making and traditional garment making. Some of the costumes I've made arguably even delve into the realms of puppetry and mask work.

I made my first suit of foam cosplay armour during my third year of university, studying Theatre Design. We were allotted two fully self-guided projects in our third year and I saw this as the perfect opportunity to use the knowledge and skills that I had learned studying theatre design to make something that I had always wanted to – a full on, head to toe Transformers suit.

I jumped right in at the deep end, deliberately picking the most complex character design I could think of. I decided that, yes, my first cosplay armour project would indeed be the Sparkeater – the monstrous, decrepit character with a complicated design of jagged, rusted plating torn away to reveal cables and wiring, who only appeared in two issues of one comic series before dying. Because that's the sort of person I am. Hypocritically enough, I usually encourage first time armour and prop makers to try out something simple first and work their way up. But if there's one thing I've learned from cosplaying, it's that cosplayers never follow our own advice.

It was a hugely challenging project - deliberately so - and I found that I fell in love with the process of working with foam, in a way that I had never felt when working with fabric. Even though I felt like I had a knack for working with foam, I still messed up, remade pieces and rethought entire methods of making parts of the costume. I got lost in the creative problem solving and spent many months happily experimenting, learning what worked for me and what didn't. Looking back on that costume now, there's so much I would do differently. I've even scrapped bits of it for parts, so if I ever wanted to wear it again I would have to improve on it. But, I still feel that my Sparkeater cosplay was both

43

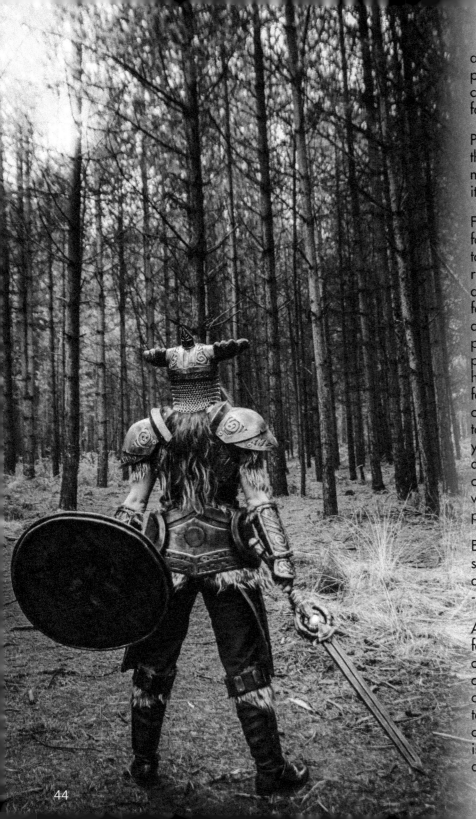

a huge achievement and a great learning process; one that reignited my passion for cosplay and sparked a new love for foam fabrication and armour crafting.

Plastazote foam was my material of choice for the majority of armour making, and still is for many reasons – cost, accessibility, the fact that it's lightweight, and especially for its versatility.

Foam can be constructed, carved, heat formed, textured, painted and weathered to look like almost anything. It can create rigid edges and complex curves, harsh battle damage and elegant decoration. It's perfect for making metallic looking surfaces, but can also be used to create more organic looking products – such as carving in a wood grain pattern, or pressing crumpled up foil into heated foam to make it look like leather. Some foams are even used in the puppetry craft to create all sorts of creatures. It's also possible to make costumes that create the illusion of your body being hugely exaggerated or a different shape entirely. This is great for cosplaying from comics and video games, where characters will often have exaggerated proportions and distinctive silhouettes.

Earlier I likened working with foam to sculpting. This versatility is what gives foam - and the process of armour making in general - that quality.

Another great advantage to working with foam is the different thicknesses that sheets of foam are available in. Using different sizes of foam for different parts of a costume can create a lot of depth, and enables the maker to consider what function different parts of a costume would serve – for example, is it functional protective plating, or finely decorated ceremonial armour? What sort of

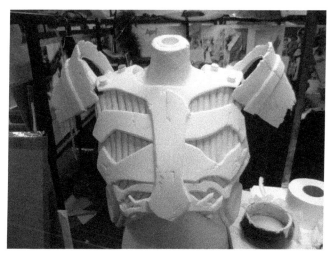

material is it supposed to be made from – whether real or fictional? Many designs will boast a variety of parts with different purposes, from pure function to ornate decoration and everything in between. Depicting different motifs with different materials, thicknesses of foam or textures, and being consistent with these choices, can add real depth and realism to a costume.

Examining costume designs in this manner also aids in better understanding of why a costume was designed the way it was, which can be both fun and useful to think about when approaching a cosplay. A good costume design tells you everything you need to know about the character who wears it and the world they live in, and also reflects the way in which they need to physically function in their clothing. When starting a cosplay I always think about what function the costume is meant to serve for the character, why certain design choices were made

because of that, and how I can best use the materials at my disposal to depict these themes and variations within the design.

At the time of writing this article, I'm working on a cosplay of Aloy from Horizon Zero Dawn; a game which boasts some of my favourite design work pretty much ever. Costumes in Horizon Zero Dawn are a fascinating blend of two opposing elements: The resources and fabrication techniques of the tribal societies in which the humans live, and the plating and components they pick off the technologically advanced machines they hunt to use for armour and weapons, and decorative items like jewellery.

The costumes are designed in such a way that you can place what armour pieces came from which machines and even why they were chosen for that purpose. For example, the Nora Lookout outfit that I'm making is one of Aloy's stealth-enhancing costumes, meant to evoke the role of a scout type. So the armour pieces

on it are taken from the machines' equivalent of a scout, the Watcher. She wears a piece of a Watcher's helm on her head. This serves as practical protection, but also reflects what the costume is meant to represent thematically. Lore-wise, you can also see how it might camouflage her while sneaking around near machines, if they saw a Watcher's head bobbing through tall grass rather than a stalking human. Around her neck she wears a Watcher's eye, which is there for decoration, but still serves a thematic purpose in the overall design, especially when placed just below the helmet on Aloy's body, evoking the head of a Watcher superimposed over Aloy's.

The juxtaposition of natural, rougher fabrics with advanced machinery, and Aloy's status as a hunter and warrior are the main things I think about when approaching this cosplay. I want the materials I choose to contrast well against each

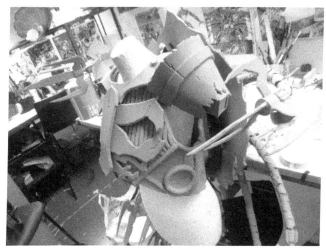

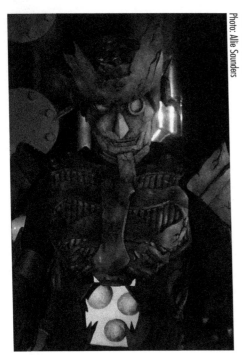

Photo: Allie Saunders

My Dragonborn cosplay that was photographed for this issue represents a warrior's armour rather than a scout's. The broad, distinctive silhouette and thick protective plating is given some Fantasy-setting elegance by the curved lines and decorative Nordic-inspired patterns. Layering pieces was important for this costume, just as with Aloy, but here the challenge was more in creating depth and definition but retaining harmony between the shape of the pieces and the embellishment patterns using texture and recessing patterned segments, rather than stacking multiple layers on top of each other.

This aim for depth also tied into my choices when it came to the other materials involved in the costume – the fur with its two-toned fade, the rough linen of the clothes, and using real steel rings to weave chainmail. The paintjob was also important for achieving this look. Dry brushed silver over darker colours made for a shiny steel finish with some depth to it. Then adding rust colours and black in the recesses and battle damage scratches to really make the details stand out.

Usually I'm a proponent of keeping battle damage on armour pretty subtle, unless the costume *really* calls for it. Sparkeater took the concept of battle damage to a whole new level. He has an extremely worn down design, where parts of his plating are broken and torn away to reveal cables underneath. I was always working in multiple layers for this

build. It's also a great example of a cosplay that requires some artistic licence on the part of the maker, as I was essentially having to imagine what each piece of armour looked like before it was damaged while planning how I would make each piece. Usually each piece of armour consisted of at least a base layer, a bunch of wires and cables, and the broken plating on top.

Another big challenge of Sparkeater - and my other Transformer Nautica - was the fact that they aren't people wearing armour, but essentially a person made from armour. For these sorts of builds - mechs, rigs, whatever you prefer to call them - scale and proportion is even more important. One thing anyone who

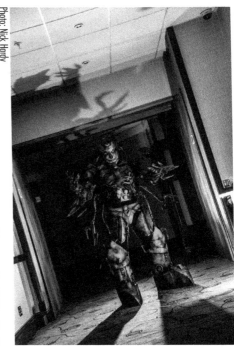

Photo: Nick Hardy

other, both in colour and texture. The fabrics, generally, are simple, colourful and natural or human-made, while the armour is complex, machine-made and bright white but with hints of metallic sheen.

The armour requires multiple layers of foam to create the look of the machines, which in-lore, are built using something akin to huge-scale automated 3D printing. Finish-wise, the armour has a look of brilliant white, but up close you can see some of the paint scraped and scratched away from use to reveal the metal underneath – achieved by painting the pieces a metallic silver first and then masking bits off before spraying them white for a smooth finish with scratches that reveal metal underneath.

makes mech type costumes quickly realises is that it's very easy to accidentally make the head of the costume completely out of proportion with the rest of it and end up with a massive bobble head.

If the character is essentially human shaped and proportioned, as most Transformers are, a general rule I follow is to exaggerate the size of the rest of the costume but make the head snug. But the easiest way to avoid the dreaded bobble head is to keep an overall vision of the costume in mind at all times, even while working on the smallest detail.

At the planning stage I'll draw a full mock-up, as I would with a large scale prop or set build, to work out how each piece of the costume will scale beside each other, as well as to my own body, and finally how they'll fit together and function as a moving, wearable costume. Having a reference like this to revisit at different stages of the making process, even if you need to revise it as you go along, is incredibly useful for large scale or oversized builds – such as costumes involving stilts.

As much as I enjoy the overall process of armour making, my favourite part of any build is always the finish – the texturing, painting and weathering which is so integral to showing the history of your costume and the character who wears it. This is where a maker can really add their own flare to a cosplay. Do you want to make your armour look as realistic as possible, or stylised like a cartoon or video game graphics? Are you going for a smooth, clean, perfect finish, or has your character accumulated a ton of battle damage, dirt and grime on their travels?

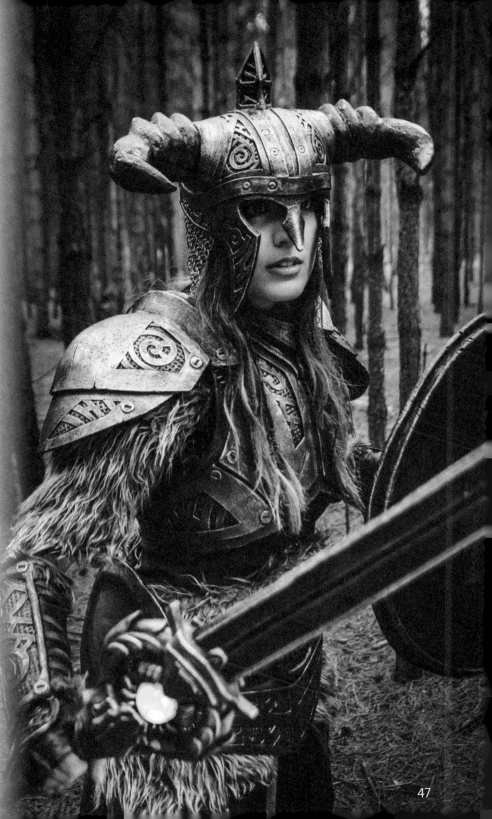

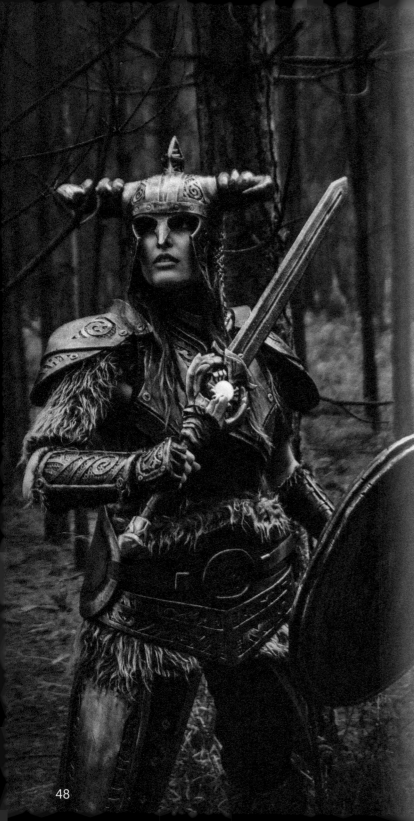

There are unique challenges to each of these things. Often the character design will dictate the best way to finish your armour. But even then there are multiple ways of achieving the same look, and there's always room to play around and interpret a costume in your own way. Some makers have a distinctive painting style, completely reinterpret characters, or design their own costumes based on a particular concept, or fusion of concepts.

I've mainly focused on crafting armour with foam as that's usually my main material of choice. But, of course, there are plenty of materials other than foam that are used to make costume armour, from cardboard to thermoplastics, and 3D printing. There are pros and cons to every option, and most of the time someone's material of choice will come down to personal preference.

The great advantage of having all of these different materials at our disposal is that a maker can combine multiple materials and techniques together in a single build, such as making armour from foam and covering it with thermoplastic, or making the majority of a costume from foam and 3D printing certain elements of it that are more suited to that process. Armour making is also ripe for combining with other fabrication skills, such as sculpting, mold making and casting, woodwork, sewing, leather work, or weaving chainmail. There are usually multiple ways to tackle any costume, and each maker will have their own preferences and skills learned through both successes and failures.

The fact that we have ever-growing access to incredible resources both online and in books, as well as a wider variety of materials, some now catered specifically to cosplay, means that the opportunity for experimentation has never been easier for cosplayers.

Cosplay is about having fun above anything else, but it's also a form of artistic expression, and a way of learning and honing a wide array of creative skills.

I thoroughly encourage anyone who has ever thought that they might like to make a suit of cosplay armour to just try it out. Whether you're already accomplished in other types of costume making, or armour would be your first foray into cosplay, seriously, just choose a costume, do some research, and go for it. I guarantee that you'll learn a lot and have a ton of fun along the way.

Isa Shaw-Abulafia

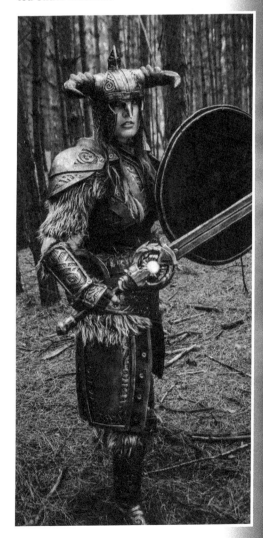

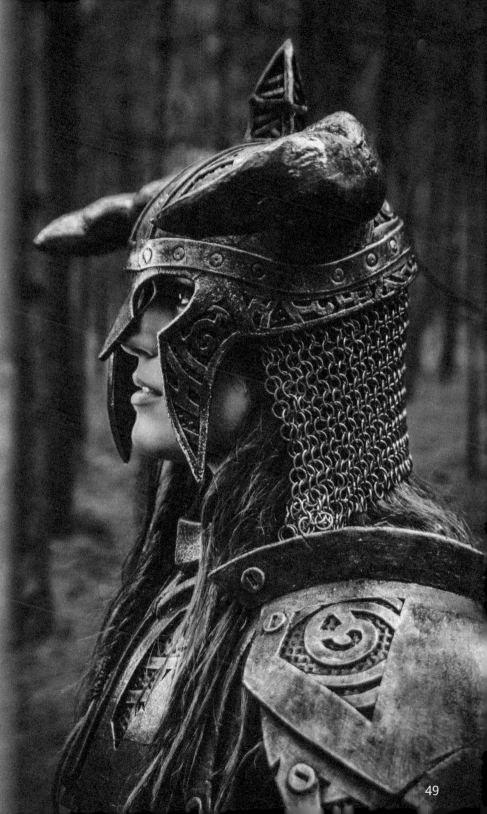

49

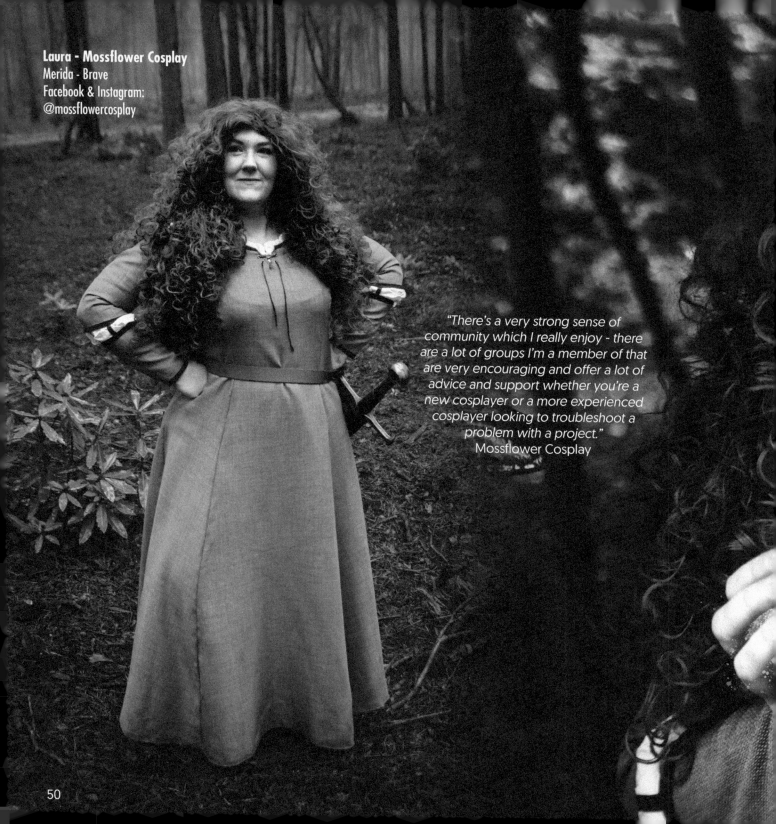

Laura - Mossflower Cosplay
Merida - Brave
Facebook & Instagram:
@mossflowercosplay

"There's a very strong sense of community which I really enjoy - there are a lot of groups I'm a member of that are very encouraging and offer a lot of advice and support whether you're a new cosplayer or a more experienced cosplayer looking to troubleshoot a problem with a project."
Mossflower Cosplay

Merida

The Cosplay Survival Guide

Going to a convention in cosplay is the most fun, it's great to show off your new and favourite costumes, but how can we make sure it all gets there safe and sound? As cosplayers we often have *a lot* of stuff after all. Here at The Cosplay Journal we thought we'd put together a handy little guide to packing your costume!

MAKE A CHECK LIST

It seems so obvious but the best way to make sure you don't forget anything for a convention is to make a check list of everything you need. You can make separate ones for each costume, one for general costume supplies, like makeup, wig nets, hair spray and the rest, and then one for your "civvie" stuff (clothes, PJs, money, etc). It really helps if you can tick off each thing as it goes in the case and you don't need to panic if you can't remember, you can just check your list.

Packing – The Essentials

There are some things that are essential for any convention trip, and you will want to bring every time no matter what costume you're wearing. When putting these little kits together you'll want to have bags/boxes to put things in so they don't get lost or mixed up, plus things might open/break in your case and you want to protect your costumes. We've included the bags as part of our kit photos.

A First Aid/Medical Kit

Most cosplay will make you suffer a little but there are plenty of ways to avoid the pain and combat it so it doesn't ruin your weekend.

- Plasters – Rubbing your feet in uncomfortable shoes is often a problem for cosplayers so you don't want to have to deal with blisters! Plus, you never know what malfunctions might happen and unwanted blood on costumes is a bad look.

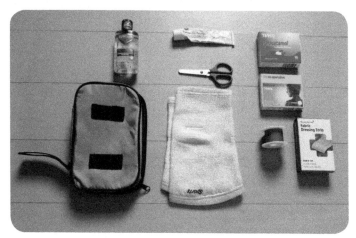

- Ibuprofen Gel – Deep Heat, Tiger Balm or just a standard Ibuprofen Gel are a must have. If you are wearing a binder you will want to sooth your shoulders at the end of the day, or if you've been on your feet all day you're legs are likely to hurt, there are plenty of reasons you might need to relax your muscles after a con.

- Pain killers – Pretty basic but you don't want your wig to be giving you a headache, or your back to be killing under the weight of your armour. If you can't take pieces of your costume off to recover (or if you have and you aren't feeling better) you are going to want pain killers. Even if the pain isn't cosplay related you don't want your day ruined.

- Knee/Elbow/Wrist supports – Little bit of an odd one and it may be you don't often need them, but having support bandages with you can really save the day. You don't want to hurt yourself with uncomfortable poses or twist your ankle in high heels.

- Scissors – For cutting plasters or the like. A must have!

- Antibacterial gel or wipes – you never know if you are going to be able to wash your   hands, so if you are taking food to a busy con where you'll be touching things all day you'll want to think about taking antibac gel or wipes with you. You don't want con-flu!

Sewing Kit

You never know when you might have a wardrobe malfunction so it's best to be prepared for all eventualities.

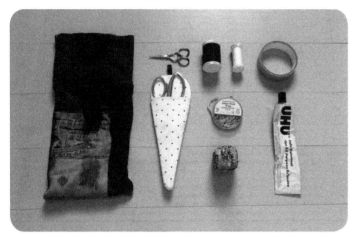

- Scissors – These are going to be ones that you do not use for your med kit! Keep them separate so you don't accidently use them for something else. You can bring fabric scissors and thread scissors if you think you might need to do more work on your costumes when you get there.

- Pins and Safety Pins – If you need to fix stuff quickly safety pins are your best bet, especially if you are already at the con (best to take some with you) but if you have a little more time pins for sewing are also good to have.

- Needles – You never know if you are going to have to stitch something!

- Thread – Bringing neutral coloured threads is always a good bet but you can also bring threads the in the colour(s) of your costume if you have space.

- Tape – Sometimes props can go wrong or break and you need a quick fix, bringing some sort of strong tape for that last minute fix can really help you out.

- Glue – For any emergency. Glue may not be the best option but sometimes it's your only option!

Food & Snacks

Convention food is often expensive so if you are trying to save your pennies you may want to bring your own food.

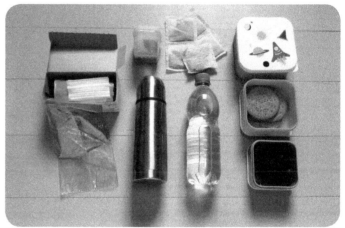

- Tea and Coffee – Hotels are likely to have tea and coffee in the room but you never know if it'll be enough, so it's worth bringing your own, especially if you want to take a flask to the con with you. You can also bring milk to store in the fridge.

- Biscuits and Dried Fruit – This is a cheap and cheerful way of making sure you keep your energy up. You can carry some with you during the day if you want to snack and not need to worry about making sandwiches or buying food at the con.

- Breakfast Bars and Crisps – A bit more expensive than biscuits and fruit but this means you won't need to pay for breakfast and you will always have something good to eat when you need it.

- Water bottle – It's a good idea to carry a drink with you at a convention; you don't want to get dehydrated!

- Flask – Having hot drinks with you at Autumn/Winter events is a great idea. We all know that cosplay isn't always weather appropriate and having something to warm you up will make your day so much better.

- Snack boxes and sandwich bags – For carrying your snacks or, if you are more prepared, sandwiches and picnic food.

Wash Kit

A wash kit does seem like an obvious thing to bring but sometimes it's worth covering all the bases, especially because a wash kit isn't just to make sure you don't smell, it can also mean feeling human again after a day at the con.

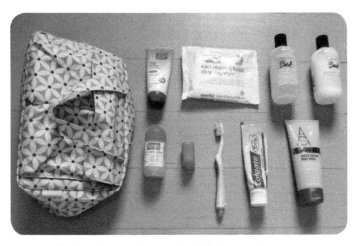

- Tooth brush, tooth brush holder and tooth paste – Ok, this is really obvious but the amount of people who forget one of these things in a rush is ridiculous. Always worth double checking!

- Deodorant – You may want to buy a new one for your con so you know it's not going to run out and make sure it's strong. You sweat a lot in cosplay and you don't want to stink out your new costume!

- Make up wipes (or your preferred makeup remover) – Looking after your skin is really important, and when you can be wearing body paint, prosthetics or even just heavy makeup all day you are going to want something you know will do the job of taking it all off afterwards without damaging your skin (too much).

- Moisturiser – To follow your makeup remover and to use before you put your makeup on. Your skin can get really dry from a day in a convention centre with heavy makeup, so make sure you're being good to yourself.

- Shampoo and conditioner – Beat wig hair at the end of the day or help get your hair under a wig net in the morning.

- A good shower gel or bubble bath – This isn't just about getting all the con grime and cosplay sweat off, relaxing your body and having some me time is super important after a full day in costume. It's good for body and mind. It's important to be able to chill after a con and making time for self-care in your convention schedule is a must.

Extra Bits & Bobs

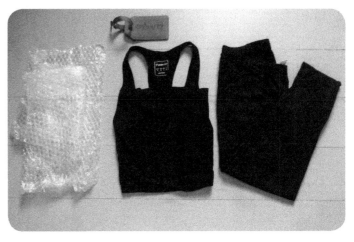

- Bubble wrap – For wrapping up props or delicate parts of your costume.

- Base layers – Wear these under you costumes. A great way to keep you warm in the winter and stop you making your costumes all sweaty in the summer.

- Luggage tag – Just in case you need to store you case at a hotel or cloak room.

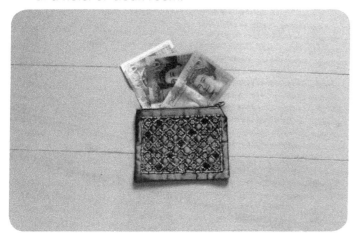

And last but not least, cash! Queues at cash points are normal at cons and sometimes they run out of money completely so if you want to buy merch or food it's a good idea to already have some on you.

How To Pack

Everyone has their own way of packing their costumes but this is a basic guide with some hints and tips for new and old cosplayers alike.

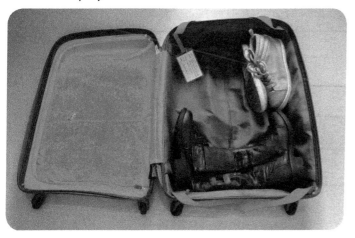

- Cases with sections (half and half) are really great for packing for a con as you can pack costumes safely and not have to worry about things moving around, especially if they have zip compartments, plus you can pack your costumes in separate compartments. We also recommend hard shell cases to add the little extra protection when travelling.

- Shoes in first – make sure boots are overlapping and lain flat so they take up as little space as possible, smaller shoes like trainers or pumps can be put in the corners or the sides, again making them as small as you can.

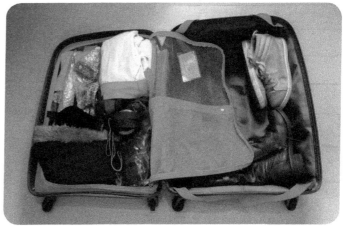

- Fold your costumes neatly – you can fold up large pieces (like this jumpsuit) to be pretty small, if you fold them neatly you can avoid creasing them too much though it's inevitable that they will crease somewhat in transport (don't worry, you can iron and hang costumes when you get to the hotel!).

- Store all the pieces of one costume together – not always doable but it's helpful to keep all the pieces together so you can pack and unpack easily. This is especially useful if you have belts, bracers or other smaller pieces with your costume so you know you've packed everything (check each piece off your check list as you put them in the case).

- Rolling costume pieces – with pieces like shirts and trousers you can roll them to make them smaller, and it helps them crease less! Unlike like a large piece like a jumpsuit or a coat, shirts, skirts and the like can be rolled and not get bulky so it's a great way to save space.

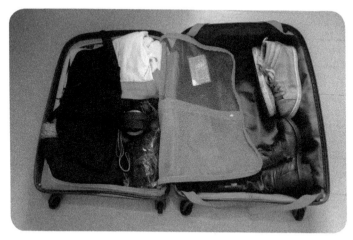

- Fold your cloaks – Cloaks are pretty big but many can be folded down to be smaller and fit nicely in your case. If you have a big cloak you can fold it and put in last over the top of everything else, which will also help protect props and costume pieces.

- Packing your accessories – pack your accessories tight and layer them on top of other pieces. If you have things like unstyled wigs or hairpieces pack them into bags so they don't get tangled, lost or damaged. Anything like arm/leg wraps, bandages or putties you will want to roll them up tight and secure them before you put them in the case.

- Wrap your props – small and delicate props are always a worry but wrapping them in bubble wrap and placing them in the case with your soft costume pieces will keep them safe in most cases. You can bury them in layers of clothes to make doubly sure.

- Belts and jewellery – putting your jewellery loose in your case is not a great idea so putting them in a little bag or a pouch inside the case (if it has one) will mean they are safe and sound. You can also wrap up your belts and put them in a bag too.

- Put any extra pieces on top – wow that's two costumes fitted in one side of the case! Smart packing and everything is protected! Obviously with bigger costumes you are going to take up more room and armour may need a box or case of its own (something we will cover in the future).

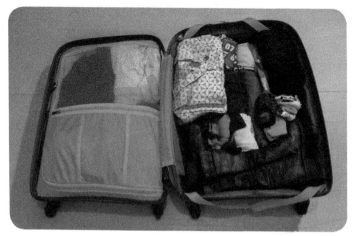

- Being able to zip that side up and keep it all tightly packed in makes all the difference. Now onto packing the rest of your stuff!

- Your wash kit may be the biggest thing to go in so get that in first and pack the rest of your stuff around it. You should also put another pair of shoes in at this point if you are bringing some, again they are bigger and you'll want to pack around them.

- Pack your "normal" clothes, PJS and underwear in next. Rolling them up will help conserve space and mean you can bring some more items. Bringing comfy, lounging around clothes is a good idea after a day in costume (self-care!).

- Put your other "kits" in next. Med and sewing kit are likely to be flat(ish) so those can go on top of everything easily and you can put your food, snack boxes (these ones stack inside each other, definitely recommend!), flask and water bottle (if it's empty, if not put it in your day bag/rucksack, don't want it leaking) in now as well.

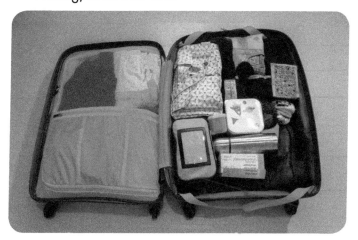

- Put any big jumpers, hoodies or coats on top to secure and protect your stuff and zip/lock the straps down.

- Close it up and you're pretty much ready to go!

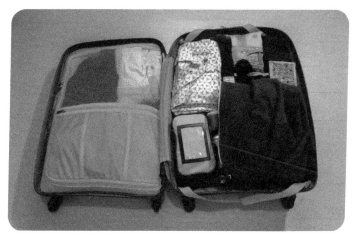

Bigger Props

If you have bigger props (or ones that are just a little too large for your case) you are probably going to want to pack them up differently to keep them safe. Items like helmets, wigs and large scale weapons are never going to be the easiest parts to pack and travel with but there are a few things you can do to make it better.

- With swords, spears, large guns or the like you will want to wrap them in bubble wrap and then in a black bin bag or tarp taped securely shut. You don't want to be getting in trouble for carrying a weapon in public or have your expensive props/ hard work ruined.

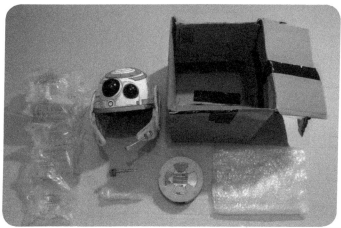

- Helmets and wigs can be stored in a box (easy to get hold of packing boxes on eBay for cheap and they flat pack for storage), using large bubble wrap or packing bubbles to stop them moving around in the box and help them keep their shape. With helmets and armour, wrap them up separately and place them in the box so that they can't shift. If you want to take a wig head you can get bigger sizes of box.

And that's it! You've got the packing basics; you and your costume are ready to survive the con!

If you have any tips you'd like to share with the cosplay community let us know on our Twitter: @cosplayjounal or Facebook: @thecosplayjournal

Holly Rose Swinyard

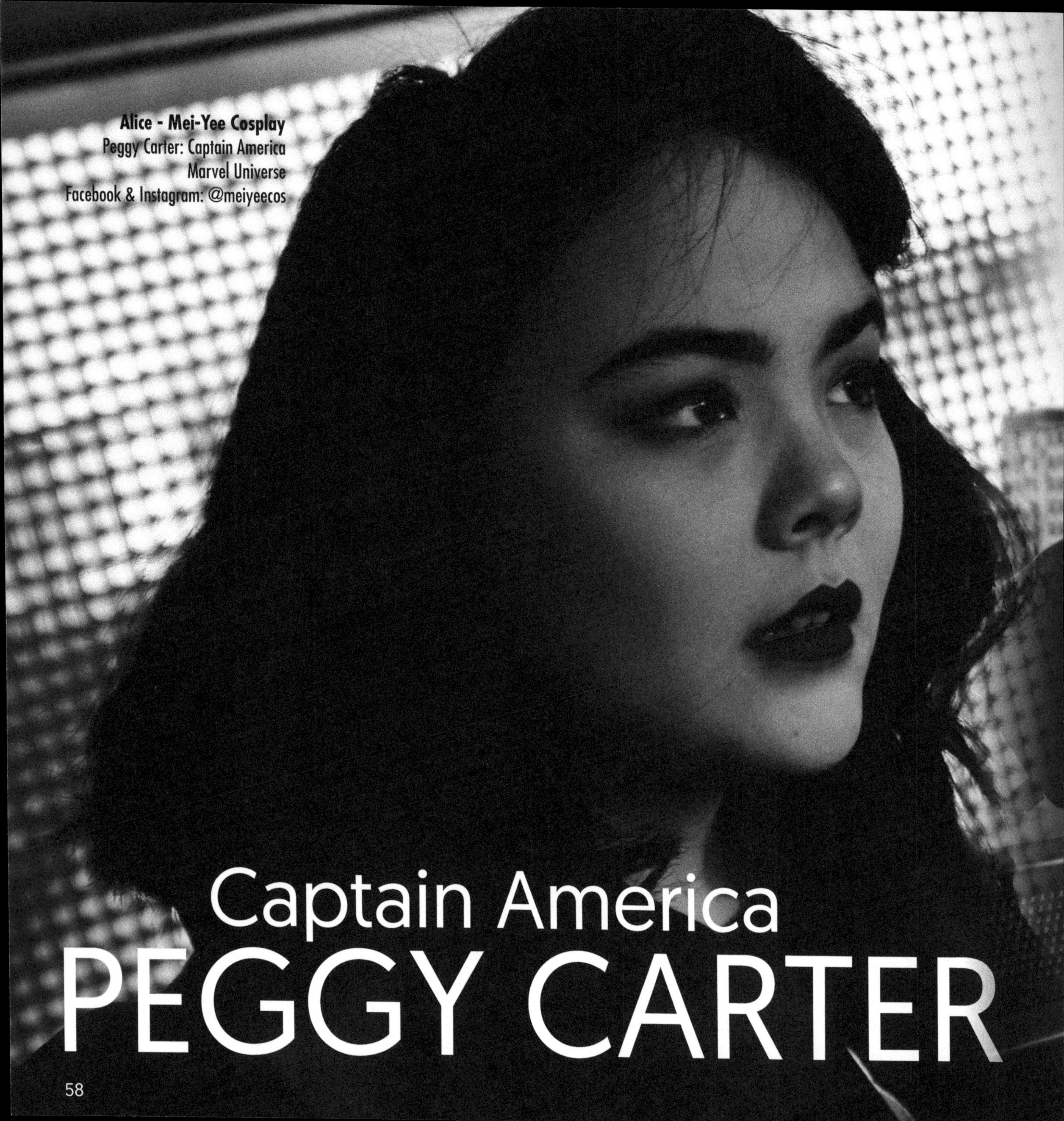

Alice - Mei-Yee Cosplay
Peggy Carter: Captain America
Marvel Universe
Facebook & Instagram: @meiyeecos

Captain America
PEGGY CARTER

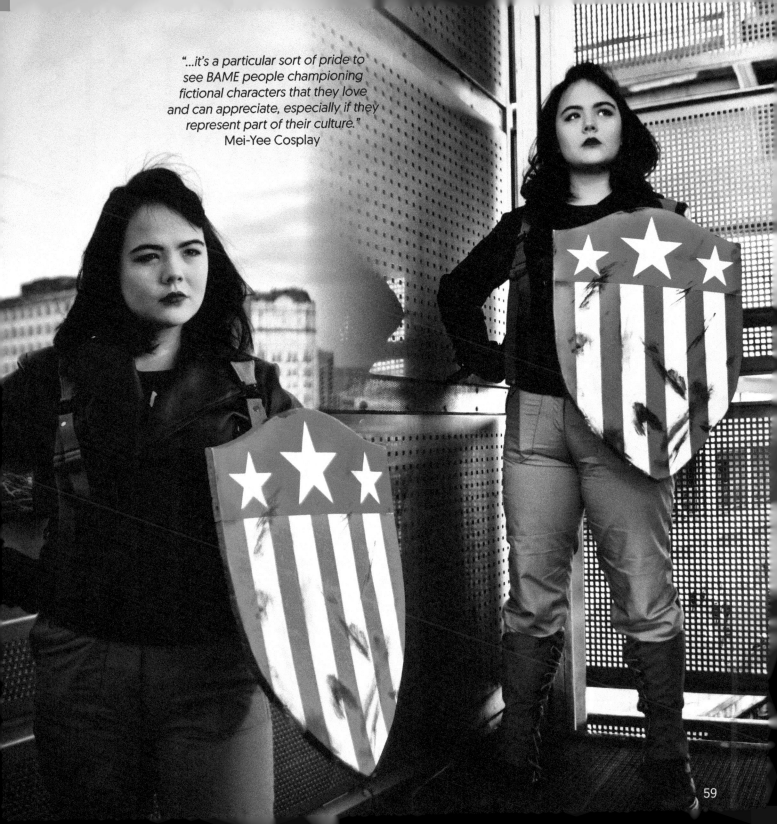

"...it's a particular sort of pride to see BAME people championing fictional characters that they love and can appreciate, especially if they represent part of their culture."
Mei-Yee Cosplay

COSPLAY GUESTS
Are They Worth It?

I'm going to start this article by being honest about any potential bias in my opinion piece. I run a cosplay zone and charity fundraising group called *Just Becos*, created in January 2016, with my boyfriend. A few months before, back in 2015 in fact, I was a cosplay guest at Bournemouth Comic Con and since that experience I have also helped at other cosplay areas with a number of groups who also provide cosplay zone services. I have a multitude of friends and acquaintances who have been cosplay guests so I'd like to make it clear that this is not on attack on any specific person/group of people/organisers of comic cons. Within this article I wish to explore my own opinions of the role of cosplay guests, which has been formed by my experiences, facts and anecdotes from those I'm close to. With all of this disclosed and the caveats given out, let's get down to the meat of the topic. We need to talk about the presence of booked cosplay guests at comic cons.

A cosplay guest is pretty much like any other booked guest at a comic con. They get a table somewhere in the comic con where they can sell prints and anything else they may have on offer. Sometimes that is all the guest does. Sometimes they give a talk on a topic relating to their particular specialities, judge a cosplay masquerade or host the masquerade itself. It very much depends on what has been agreed between the cosplay guest and the organisers of the comic con. If they are involved with the cosplay masquerade as a judge or host that would also be agreed with whoever is running the masquerade.

If it seems like they don't do all that much, that is because they don't. On its face there's a distinct lack of interactivity or stimulating activities on offer when a random cosplayer is sat at a table with merchandise and a pen in their hand. When I have been a guest before I found the times where I was just sat at my table incredibly dull. I was twiddling my thumbs, hoping that someone would spot me and buy one of my hastily printed prints. I found myself jumping at the opportunity to speak to cosplayers who went by, compliment their costume and suggest they enter the cosplay masquerade later in the day. It meant I had a chat with people that weren't just people I knew who were working in the same area as me. It was at times demoralising and at others just plain boring. The main source of enjoyment was judging the masquerade with two other cosplay guests - Heartbound Cosplay and Riddikulus Cosplay - and seeing all the brilliant entries that graced the stage. The main source of my enjoyment was barely any different from any event where I came as an attendee as opposed to a guest. I cannot speak for the other cosplay guests, but my presence there felt a little bit perfunctory. I could've easily been replaced by another cosplayer ideally based closer to the local area.

A part of me has to question the logic of having cosplay guests at comic cons, especially at local ones. Generally speaking, cosplay guests bring very little in terms of return of investment. You may be fooled into thinking that they have a fanbase that may come along to your comic con but it rarely translates to reality unless you book an honest to God celebrity like Yaya Han or Jessica Nigri. I understand why certain cosplayers may be booked, especially over someone who may be a bit more local. An organiser may see the number of likes on someone's page and go, "Oh they have several thousand likes. They must be popular. I must have them in my show." The vast majority of cosplayers who have a significant number of likes on their Facebook pages or followers on Instagram are known for more than just cosplay, whether they're a model, an actor, a business owner that sells products/services relating to cosplay etc. I'd even go as far to say that there are a number of people who use cosplay as a means to extend their platform and the vast majority of their likes will come from their other work which rarely relates to their cosplay work. It shows in not only the way they interact with the cosplay community but also in the way they behave at an event they're booked at. I understand that a cosplay guest is meant to promote themselves but cosplay does not merely consist of singular, self-serving people. It's a community which is, by definition, a group of people living in the same place or having a particular characteristic in common. Is it really worth spending hundreds of pounds on an individual who'll only sit there?

With all I've said in mind, does this mean that I think cosplayers shouldn't be a part of comic cons besides as attendees? Absolutely not. There is a way in which cosplayers can be a part of the comic con that is appealing to both consumers and organisers: as part of a cosplay zone! But why, I hear you ask? Well, cosplay zones are places where people - whether they be cosplayers or not - can learn more about the hobby in a safe and inclusive environment. There are a number of things that hired cosplayers can do at a comic con that'll be of benefit to all.

Firstly, they can give talks on their chosen specialities. The talks can be quite general from Cosplay 101 or Craft in Cosplay to a specific tutorial in their area of expertise - covering more specialised topics including How to Use Body Paint, Wigs & Lenses and much more. Secondly, hired cosplayers can participate in other parts of the comic con in character. Got an Iron

Throne you want people to pay to have photos with? Why not have a Daenerys and a Jon Snow cosplayer accompany your guests in their picture for an extra couple of quid? Got a replica DeLorean? Hire a Marty McFly cosplayer to pose with guests and the car. Offer the cosplayer a cut of the profits for all of their hard work. Of course one of the most notable things hired cosplayers may be involved with at a comic cons is in the running and/or judging of cosplay masquerades. They would run a competition for other cosplayers to show off their costumes and select winners to receive prizes which can vary from merchandise to vouchers, from trophies to cash prizes.

And even if you don't have the time to hire cosplayers and oversee a cosplay area among the other comic con responsibilities, you're in luck. There are a number of groups that run cosplay areas at events. These include but are not limited to Costume & Play, The Cosplay Club and my group Just Becos. These are groups who are dedicated to creating cosplay areas that utilise their performers to provide cosplay-related activities for your attendees to enjoy throughout the day. Some of these groups do more than just provide cosplay areas, also doing charity fundraising during and aside from their cosplay zone bookings with dedicated charities they fundraise for.

The benefits of using these kinds of groups speak for themselves: they take a huge task off the hands of comic con organisers, they often have their own team ready to work and they usually have access to cosplayers who can

make the most of the money spent paying for them.

A cosplayer who wants to be paid to be involved in comic cons may look at my list of potential tasks and gawp in dismay or shock. Perhaps you think I expect too much. I don't think I do at all. I very much believe that when a cosplayer has more to offer an event, their experience has the potential to be as rewarding as the attendees who benefit from it. I and a number of cosplay zone coordinators have worked with some of the best talent on the UK scene who've not only taught others but have helped create a wonderful atmosphere. Sure, it means one would have to do some work besides waiting for someone to buy a print but it can be a gratifying experience for anyone on the crew. It warms my heart to receive messages, or be approached by attendees, who've happily told me that what they learned from the crew inspired or helped them in some way. It makes the evenings spent organising the cosplay areas after an already long day at work very much worth it.

In the end it all comes back to this inalienable truth: cosplayers who are a part of a comic con should grow the community and inspire the next generation rather than their bank accounts and social media outreach. We want acceptance from society and a space for ourselves, to make our spaces safe and allow others to come into our world by giving them a magnificent experience in the place we're most likely to meet: comic con.

Jennifer Drewett

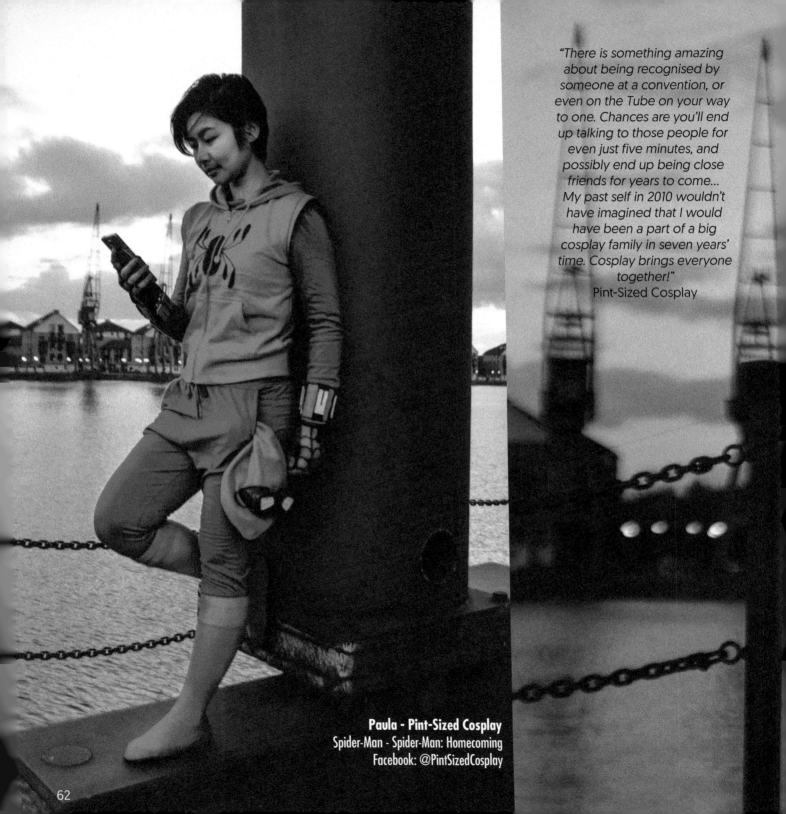

"There is something amazing about being recognised by someone at a convention, or even on the Tube on your way to one. Chances are you'll end up talking to those people for even just five minutes, and possibly end up being close friends for years to come... My past self in 2010 wouldn't have imagined that I would have been a part of a big cosplay family in seven years' time. Cosplay brings everyone together!"
Pint-Sized Cosplay

Paula - Pint-Sized Cosplay
Spider-Man - Spider-Man: Homecoming
Facebook: @PintSizedCosplay

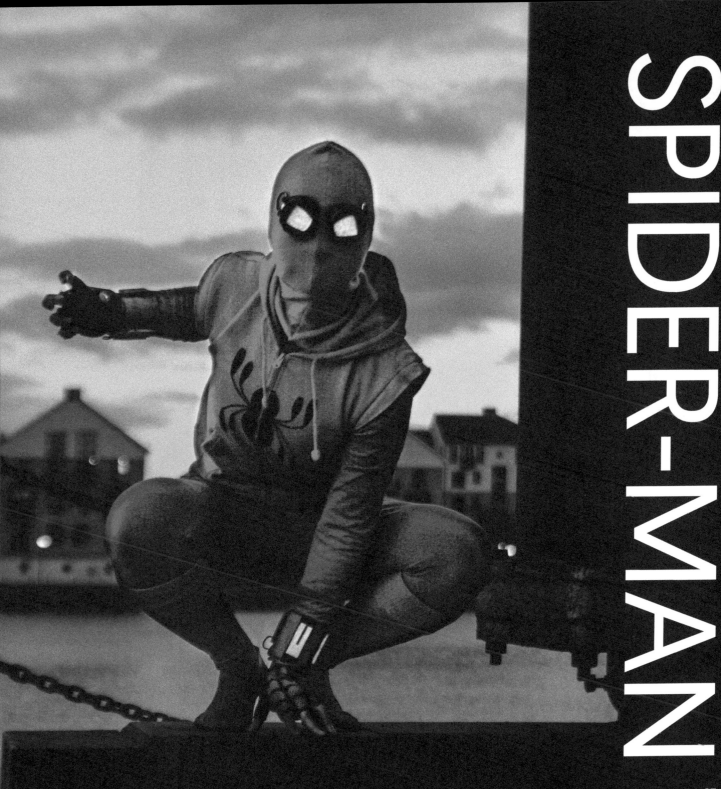

SPIDER-MAN

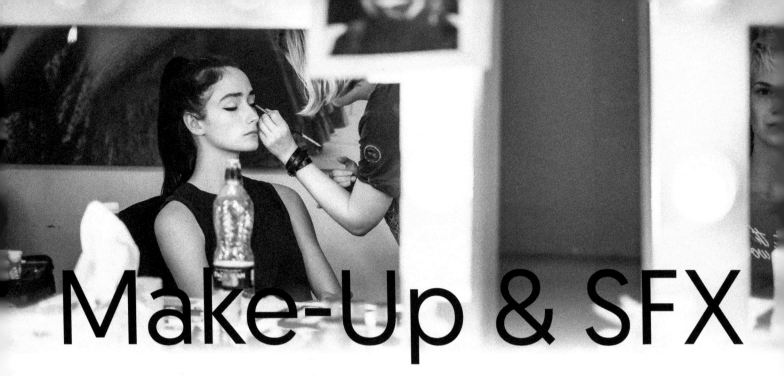

Make-Up & SFX

Featured cosplayer:

Matt - Angelophile Cosplay
Peter Pettigrew aka Wormtail - Harry Potter
Facebook: @angelophilecosplay
Instagram: @angelophileuk

As a teenager I never had much of an interest in make-up, I would always rather be making an Airfix model than working on getting the perfect brow or learning how to do a cut crease. It wasn't until I was in university that I took any interest in it at all, but it was in my second year when a friend introduced me to cosplay that I realised the true potential in make-up.

In cosplay, and in general, make up artistry can be split into two sections; Make-Up and Special Effects (SFX), although often the lines are blurred or the two are used harmoniously but for the sake of simplicity it's easier to tackle them as separate subjects. In the simplest terms make-up is what you can do with the existing structure of the face and body with colour and skin products; whereas SFX enables you to enhance and change the face and body with the help of prosthetics, appliances and masks.

Almost every cosplay will have some form of make-up, from a smattering of dirt or a slight reshaping of a key feature, through to fully painted on body art costumes and prosthetic heads. For me, make up is an essential part of cosplay, allowing cosplayers to really get into character, but it needn't be expensive or extravagant. With a plethora of tutorials available online and drug store make up constantly becoming better quality, it's becoming easier to create beautiful make up looks on a budget. This is less true for SFX where a lot of the materials are still fairly expensive but there are more "home-grown" alternatives for simpler effects.

At its simplest point make up can be used to highlight defining features of your character, (what would a Kuvira cosplay be without the thick black angled eyebrows?) or using make up products to weather the character with dirt (think Lara Croft or Ellie from the Last of Us). Building from this point the possibilities are endless.

A newer technique that I've seen adopted by cosplayers, and one that takes some fair skill to perfect, is using make up to actively change the features of the face to more accurately resemble the actor playing a character (see Maker and Muse Cosplay's recent Nancy from Stranger Things test for an excellent example). This particular technique is similar to drag make up, where contouring and shading are used to change the appearance of the face. Though it does have some drawbacks, looking fantastic at certain angles, with certain lighting and especially on camera but it can look unwieldy and unflattering in other lights. In a similar vein many cosplayers use make up to change their appearance so that they look more like the character's gender. Stubble, contouring harsher features and drawing in thicker eyebrows can make a female face look more masculine, see our distinguished editor Holly Rose, aka Lilprince, for a fine example. Of course men can also use drag make up to appear more feminine, like the brilliant Ross Cobbold, aka RossECobb, although arguably it is more difficult for a man to look convincingly feminine, there are of course exceptions to this rule, see Richard Arthur, aka TheOfficialAriel.

Arguably the most technically difficult make up that a cosplayer can master is Body Art, although for reasons of modesty at conventions this is usually more Body-Suit Art. The most popular example of this is Mystique from the X-Men franchise. I've seen some beautiful examples of this (see Nadya Sonika's cosplay by artist Lymari Millot) and some less accomplished versions. In reality this is a form of make-up that is nigh on impossible to do alone. Body Art requires covering parts of the body that you could not possibly reach alone, make up that will not rub off and application that will convincingly replicate your chosen character. It's a level of make-up that I have not attempted in cosplay and I doff my cap to anyone that can pull it off with or without professional help.

In the UK film and TV industry, as a make-up artist you are expected to also work with hair and in cosplay you can't talk about creating a look without mentioning hair. The jury is out on whether it is better to use your own hair

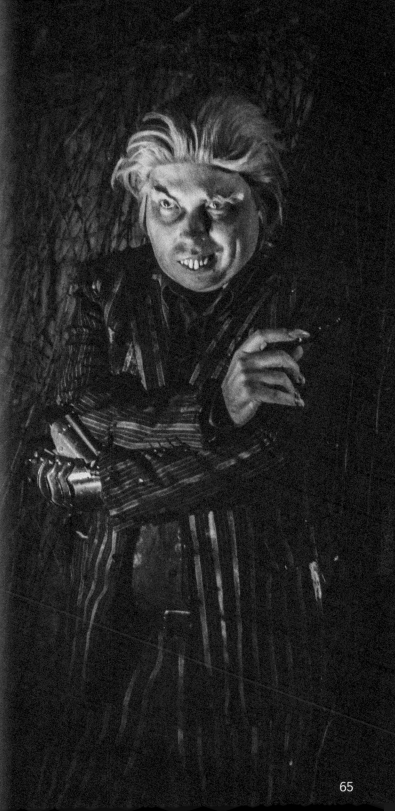

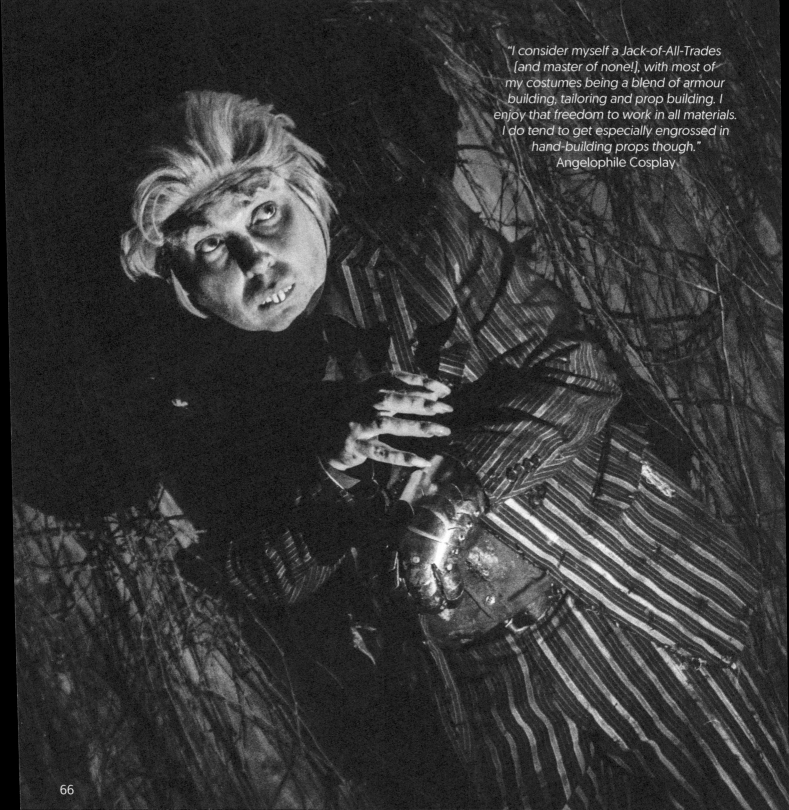

"I consider myself a Jack-of-All-Trades (and master of none!), with most of my costumes being a blend of armour building, tailoring and prop building. I enjoy that freedom to work in all materials. I do tend to get especially engrossed in hand-building props though."
Angelophile Cosplay

or a wig, both have their advantages. Using your own hair will, of course, look more realistic, as you don't have to worry about blending the edge of the wig, but using a wig means that you can prepare the full style ahead of time and just apply it when you need it. A lace front (or full real hair lace but that comes with a hefty price tag) will always give the most realistic impression of hair as the lace is glued to the forehead and blended into the skin. Having said that, I've seen cosplayers do incredible things with fancy dress shop wigs and the ingenuity of the cosplay community with figuring out how to work with budget materials that are difficult to style will never cease to amaze me.

From my earliest days of cosplay, Special Effects have always been my preferred method of transforming myself. For me it is all about the creation. I've always been someone who loves to make things and SFX has a more physical effect than make up. Although there are some go-to products that any cosplayer can use, like rigid collodion for scarring or fake blood for cuts, in general SFX requires a more rigorous process than standard make up.

As a professional, I feel that it is always important to stress that although SFX can be great fun and bring amazing results, it is really important to make sure that you put in the research beforehand and are careful with the products that you choose to use, as special effects materials can be dangerous if not used properly. One of the first cosplays I worked on was Zuko, from Avatar: The Last Airbender, which required a burn scar on one side of my face. I used liquid latex and tissue paper to create the effect and it is still an effective and budget friendly way of creating this kind of effect. However anyone who's used latex knows the horrible smell, that smell is actually ammonia that is released as the latex dries, because of this it should never be applied directly to the eye area and should always be used in a well-ventilated area.

With words of warning aside, SFX can be used to completely change your appearance, from otherworldly alien transformations to scars and wounds, there is a whole world to be explored. There is always a discussion as to whether it is better to make your own SFX or commission and there are, of course, advantages and disadvantages to both. SFX materials are expensive, so commissioning an item can often be a bit of an investment, but often it does mean that the final product is of a better quality than what you could make at home. I don't buy into this idea that buying parts of your cosplay makes it any less of an achievement, safety first kids! However if you enjoy the process and are willing to put in the time it is possible to create some amazing effects from your home.

There is only one final topic I would like to touch on which doesn't get a lot of air time but to me is just as, if not more, important than any other part of make-up. Removal. I have seen, and have been guilty of this myself, so many cosplayers removing their make up with make-up wipes; as a short term solution when you're running from a convention centre to a train this is fine, but they will only do so much and leaving residue on your skin can do real damage in the long run. With SFX it really depends on what you are using but for general make-up there is one product I swear by, and that is cleansing oil. The only compound that will break down waterproof make up is oil, so when you're cleaning your face use cleansing oil and a cloth; coconut oil, sunflower oil or olive oil will not cut it, make sure you're using real cosmetic cleansing oil. The best drug store option I have found is the Simple cleansing oil. Trust me, you'll thank me later.

At the end of the day how and what you use to create your make up masterpiece is completely up to you, but don't be afraid to start. There is a whole world of tutorials and guides out there and with the make-up industry expanding every day you'd be surprised what you can do on a budget. Really, all I can say is, "Have fun!" And stay safe…

Sophia Haden

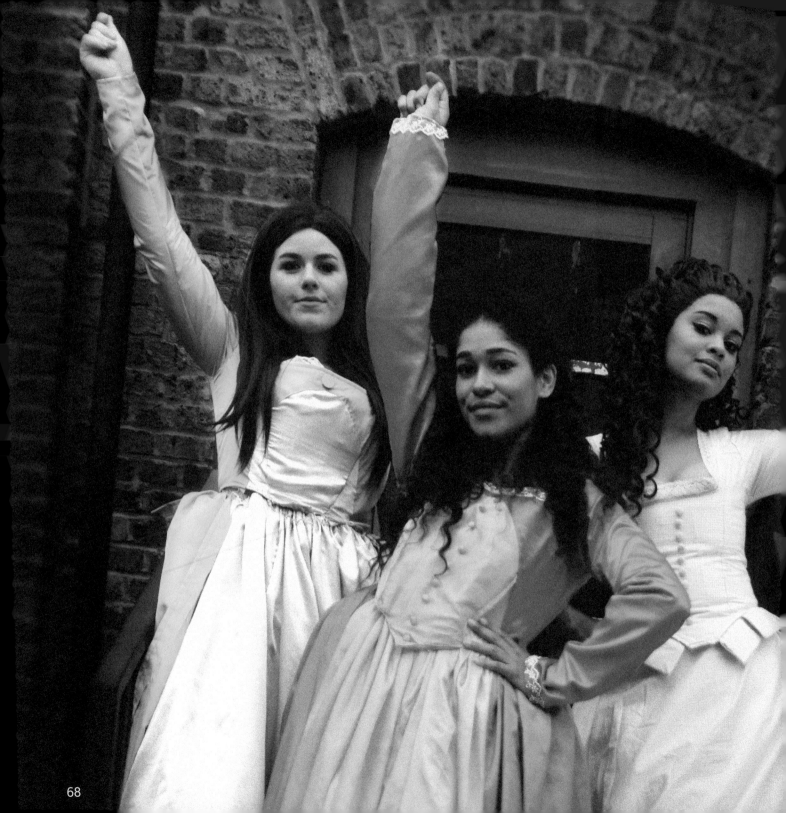

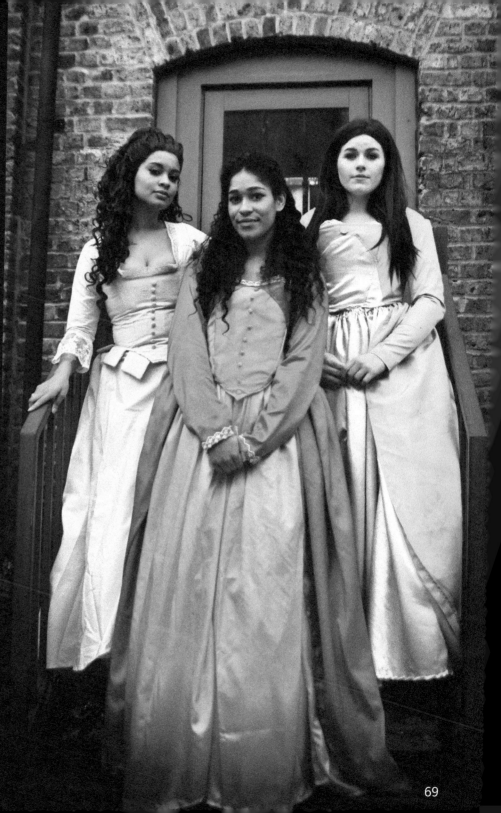

SCHUYLER SISTERS

Savanah - Wilddd Cosplay
Dani - Gathering Storm Cosplay
Imogen - Katya Cosplay Schuyler
Sisters - Hamilton
Facebook: @wildddcosplay
@gatheringstormcosplay
@katyacosplay

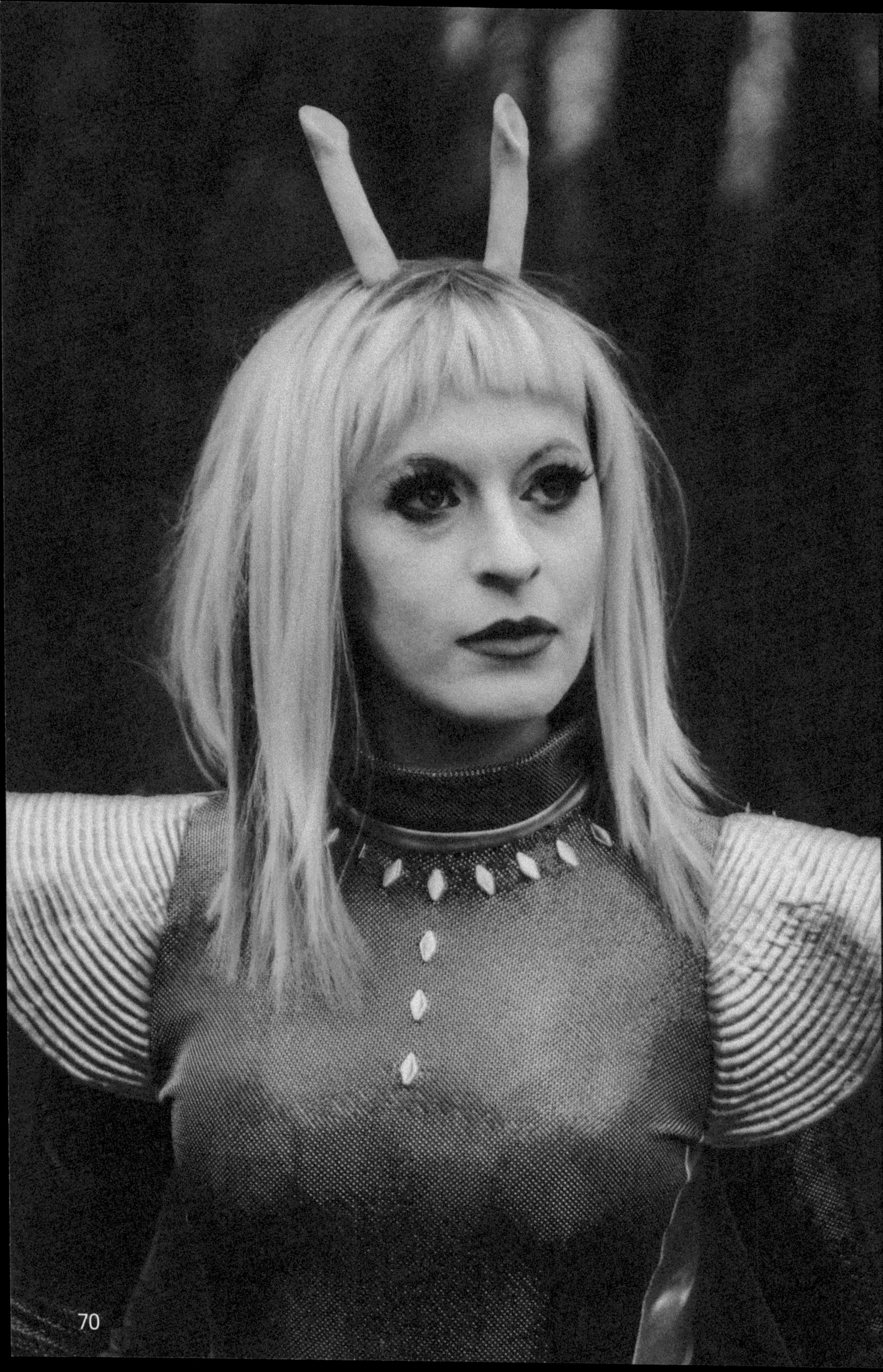

ENA WILSON

ZIZI MOONDUST

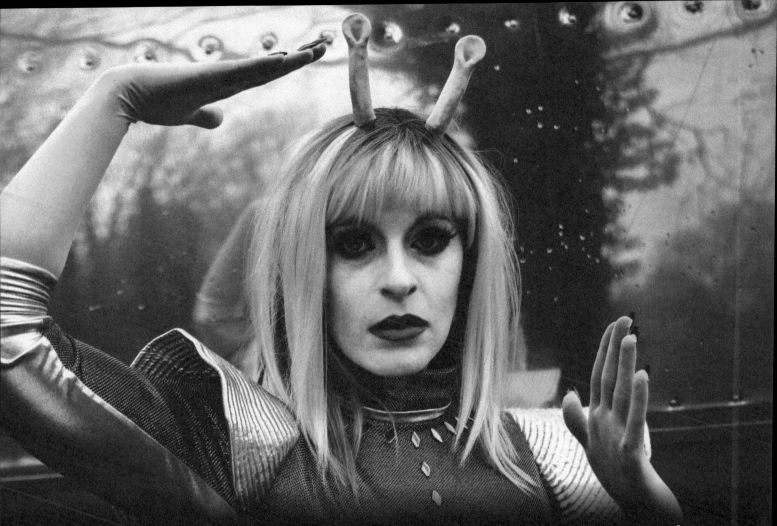

Ena Wilson, aka Zizi Moondust, styles herself as part cosplay, part drag, and all spectacular. Unlike many cosplayers she has gone about creating a single character that she can play with, build a myriad of outfits for and, as a mirror to cosplay culture, create a pastiche of current cosplay trends in the most loving and positive way; posing for selfies, photoshoots and making memes as the character Zizi. It's a fun, silly and entertaining take on the more "standard" way of cosplaying. With a background more in the area of theatrical costumes and drag, Ena has a slightly different and self-examining take on cosplay that many may not have thought about or experienced. We talked to her on location and found out all about her experiences as a cosplayer and an artist.

How did you first find out about, and get involved in, cosplay?

I've been making costumes forever. I finished college with full marks in A level theatre design, didn't get into the university I wanted to, despite the grade, apparently my portfolio was lacking anything that wasn't college work so in an attempt to bulk my portfolio out I started looking towards making reproductions of stage costumes, from CATS the musical mostly. It then lead to cosplay in general. That was in 2006. It was a downward spiral; I never applied for uni again.

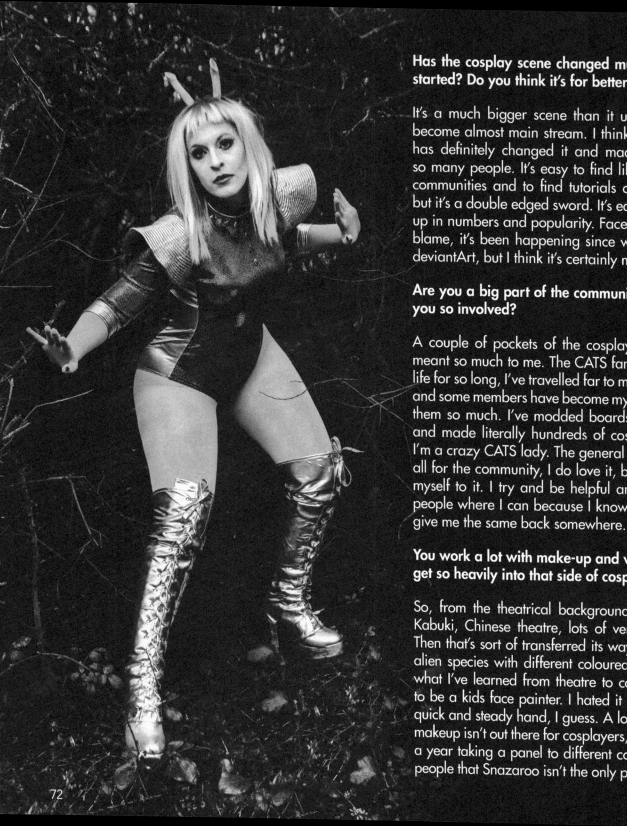

Has the cosplay scene changed much since you first started? Do you think it's for better or worse?

It's a much bigger scene than it used to be and it's become almost main stream. I think that social media has definitely changed it and made it accessible to so many people. It's easy to find like-minded people, communities and to find tutorials on how to cosplay but it's a double edged sword. It's easy to get wrapped up in numbers and popularity. Facebook isn't solely to blame, it's been happening since way back when on deviantArt, but I think it's certainly magnified it.

Are you a big part of the community? If so, why are you so involved?

A couple of pockets of the cosplay community have meant so much to me. The CATS fandom has been my life for so long, I've travelled far to meet other members and some members have become my best friends, I owe them so much. I've modded boards, created tutorials and made literally hundreds of costumes for people. I'm a crazy CATS lady. The general cosplay scene, I'm all for the community, I do love it, but I don't dedicate myself to it. I try and be helpful and encouraging to people where I can because I know that someone will give me the same back somewhere.

You work a lot with make-up and wigs, how did you get so heavily into that side of cosplay?

So, from the theatrical background and CATS came Kabuki, Chinese theatre, lots of very heavy makeup. Then that's sort of transferred its way to cosplay. I love alien species with different coloured skin. I've applied what I've learned from theatre to cosplay. I also used to be a kids face painter. I hated it but it's given me a quick and steady hand, I guess. A lot of information on makeup isn't out there for cosplayers, so I spent just over a year taking a panel to different conventions to teach people that Snazaroo isn't the only product out there!

What tips would you give to cosplayers wanting to start doing more body paint/make-up with their costumes?

Body stockings, seriously, dye them, wear them, they look like you're painted. No mess at a con. For the body, alcohol based makeup if you can, that stuff is water and rub proof, then for the face, crème based all the way. Kryolan Supracolor is my fave brand. Just having the right product to deal with the job you want it to do can make such a difference to your cosplay.

What is your favourite thing to use/work with when you are making your costumes?

Fabric! I love to sew, I try to teach myself everything and I love researching which fabric I should use for each costume. My favourite to use is organza, it's cheap, I like to double it up in different colours and then back it onto a calico or drill to make it look like a more expensive fabric. I love making corsets; the construction is surprisingly easy and so pleasing when it creates a structured shape.

You've talked about how you've struggled with cosplay in the past on your Facebook page due to issues you had with your appearance, can you tell The Cosplay Journal a bit about that and what effect it had on you?

I used to have a severe over and open bite. I'd never open my mouth or smile in photos, never eat in front of strangers; it used to hold me back all of the time. I'd still cosplay and I'd be so shy in front of a camera generally. Recently I had braces and reconstructive

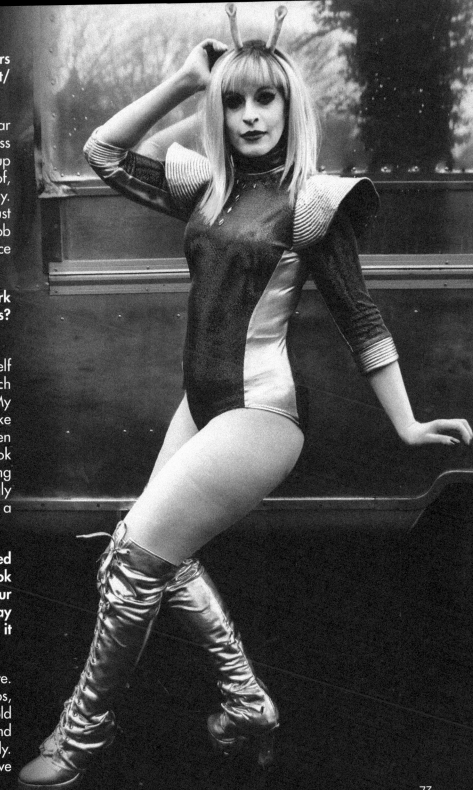

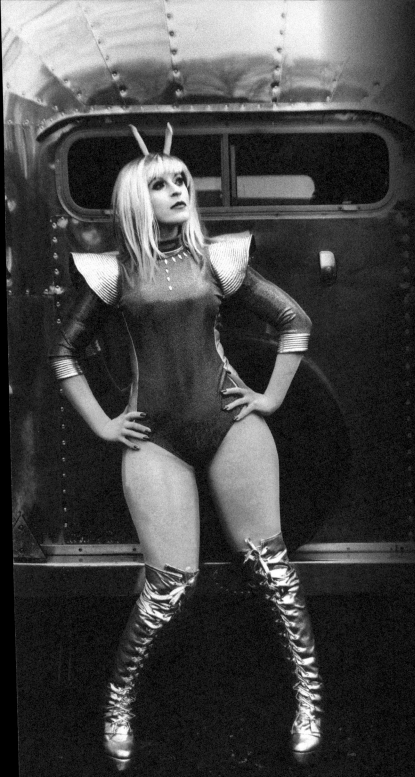

jaw surgery to fix this and I look so normal! I can smile and everything. I have to practice smiling for photos because it doesn't come naturally. Now I'm so confident because I look so normal. It's been honestly life changing.

Is there an issue with how cosplayers are treated based on their appearance?

Definitely! So many cosplayers get stick for everything from their weight and build to the fact that they've had a boob job....apparently you shouldn't enhance your appearance cosmetically.....people tell me I have a beautiful smile. I tell them to thank my surgeon.... I know some amazing plus sized cosplayers whose costumes have been stunning yet at a con are never asked for a photo. The be all and end all of cosplay is not just attention but when everyone around you is having their pic taken and nobody wants you? It's so disheartening.

Over all though do you think that cosplay has made a significant difference in your life?

It's taken over. I've been in toxic situations where I've put myself in debt, cancelled plans to finish costumes, stressed and turned up late to events and put my other half through hell so that I could get stuff done. I've been able to step back and look at myself though, I think it's important to be open and honest and say that these are bad sides to cosplay so that other people can try to avoid them. Now I limit myself as to how many costumes I make, if it's not finished for an event I'll wear something else. When something stops being fun then you have to rethink.

Finally, cosplay is for everyone, so how would you encourage people to get involved?

There are no rules. If you're into making accurate costumes, that's fantastic. You want to do original designs? Do it. You do it to give you a confidence boost? Amazing. You want to compete, meet other fans and show your love for fandom? Then do all of this. Cosplay is all of this.

If you want to find out more about Ena and Zizi follow her on:

Facebook: @ ZiziMoondust

Instagram @zizimoondust

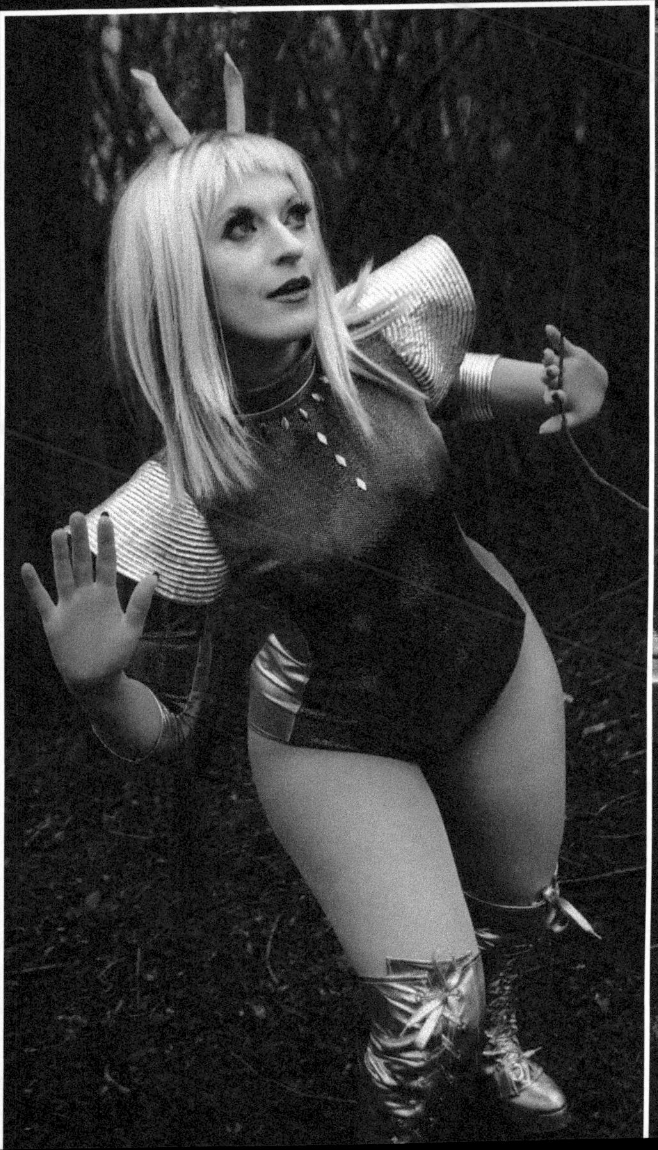

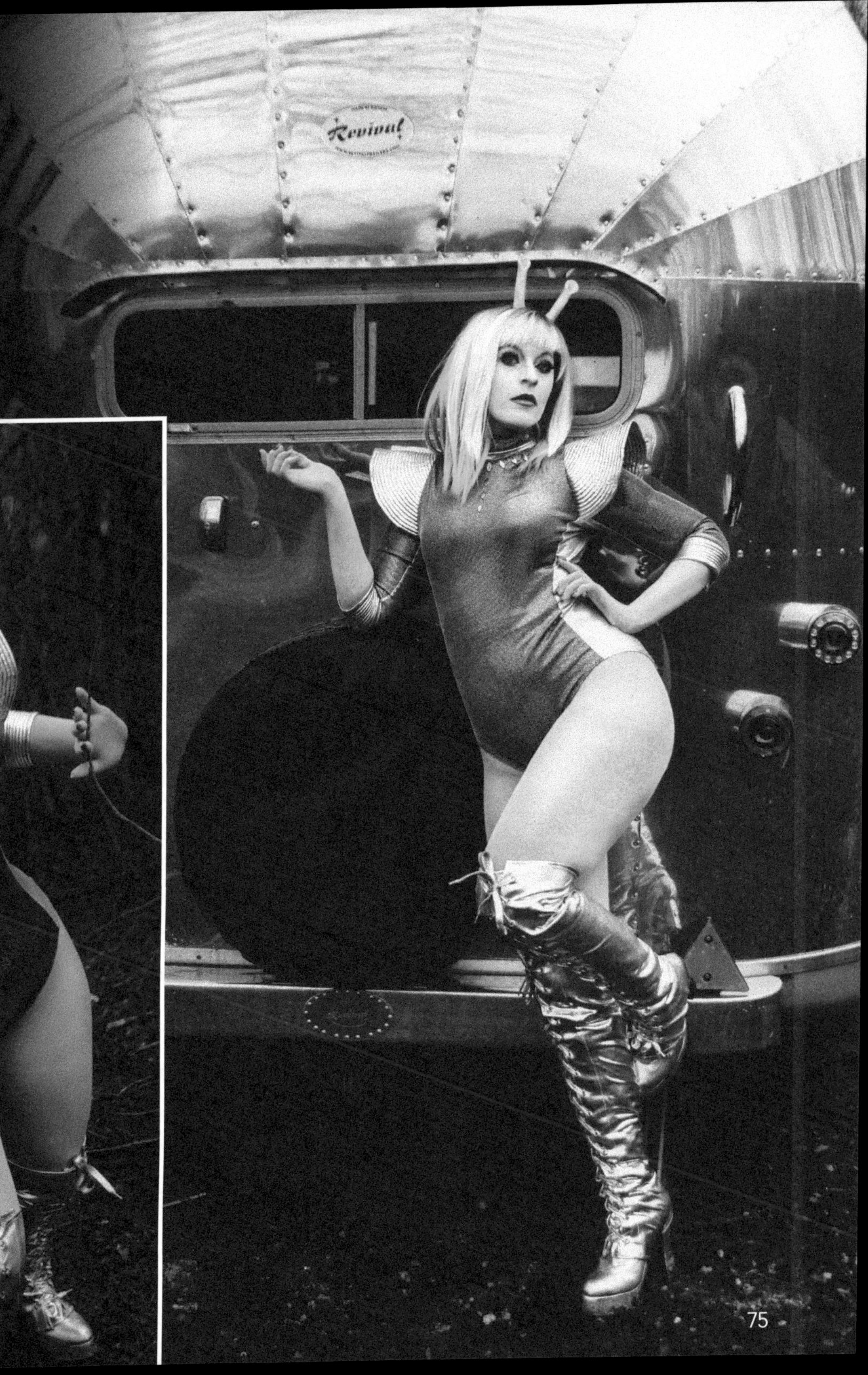

I began cosplaying in 2013, shortly after I moved to Bath from Kent in order to read History at university. I have since passed my Undergrad, I am still living in Bath, and am now finishing off a Master's. I have begun to make a small name for myself as a writer of Sci-Fi (honestly didn't see that one coming…) and I am still cosplaying. In the intervening years I've moved one and a half miles to the east of my original student house, and am now sharing a two bedroom flat with my best friend. We do not yet have a cat, but we're working on it.

Unlike many cosplayers, amateur and professional, I don't have a dedicated space or room to work on my projects. This is, perhaps, a hangover from when I made costumes in my student house. Prior to studying History, I'd had ambitions of a career in costume design, having taken both Textiles GCSE and A Level, but a very nasty bout of ill health in my final year had put paid to the idea. In 2013 I was seriously lacking a creative outlet, and the prospect of going out in fancy dress simply for the fun of it was a new and interesting concept; my only

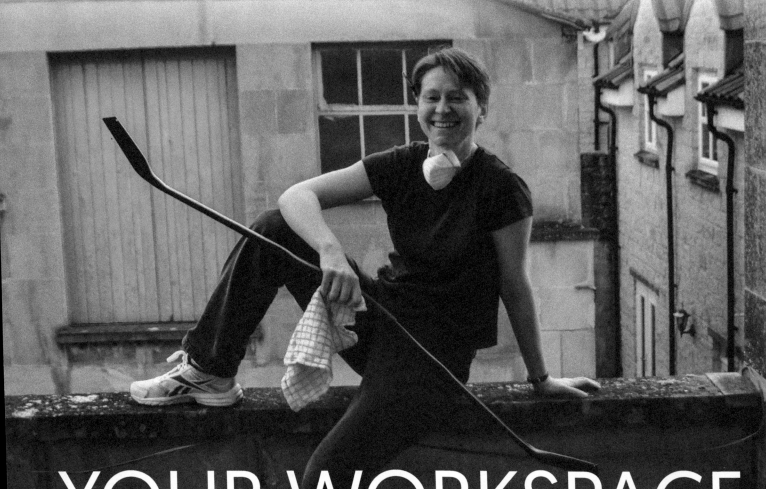

YOUR WORKSPACE

problem was a significant lack of space. I was sharing that property with four other people, and of all the rooms mine was the smallest – barely enough space to fit a single bed, a tiny desk and a chest of drawers. My wardrobe had to live on the landing. There was no communal space either, apart from the very narrow kitchen, so the three 'working surfaces' available to me were the hallway floor (cutting out), my desk (sewing machine), and my bed (small cutting-out and hand-sewing). What costumes I made were very much dictated by the space I had available. Cloaks and armour had to fold down small because, in the end, I had to make sure my stuff didn't get in anybody else's way. And, believe me, that was a challenge in itself.

Now I have much more freedom to leave projects out whilst I work on them, but it's always very much at the front of my mind that the flat is a shared space open to visitors, and as such should not be overly full or untidy with my things. It's a good work ethic, I suppose; I always know where everything is, and it's relatively easy to clean up after a project – and, as such, my flatmate is still my friend. I also have an abhorrence of clutter, so it's often very good for my stress levels that I can tuck a project neatly out of the way to work on at a later date while I get on with something else.

My primary workspace is the front room, at the sofa and coffee table. This is where I put my sewing machine, as the desk I have in my bedroom is too high and narrow to comfortably sew at. The floor here is my cutting-out surface as, by moving the coffee table to one side, I have a decent expanse of flooring to lay fabric flat and pin pattern pieces in place. Incidentally, I have become a lot better at not accidentally pinning my work to the carpet! The back of the sofa also acts as a sort of sideboard, with fabric and pattern pieces draped over its arms or high back whilst I work – within easy reach, but safely out of harm's way. Using table, sofa and floor in a complementary manner has been fairly important, as all my costumes to date have been fabric pieces, and have included large pieces such as cloaks or robes. The vast majority of my projects are therefore planned and executed in that room.

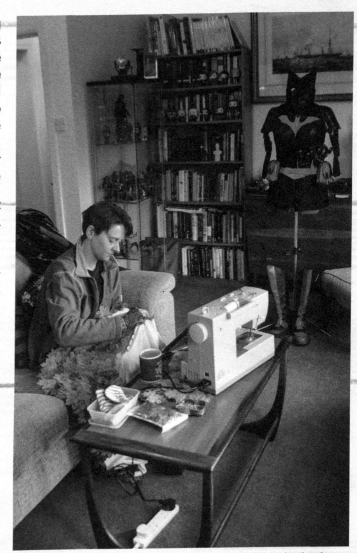

My sewing machine is a heavy-duty model, which I have dubbed "The Beastie." I really love it, because it can easily get through materials such as PVC, leather and thick calicos, whilst allowing me to sew thinner fabrics at very high speeds. It has, however, got me into trouble with my downstairs neighbours, as it does have a tendency to make their windows rattle! Happily we've worked out a standing agreement that I don't do any machine sewing past ten o'clock at night, which suits me fine. I am not really a night owl, and I plan my projects around this

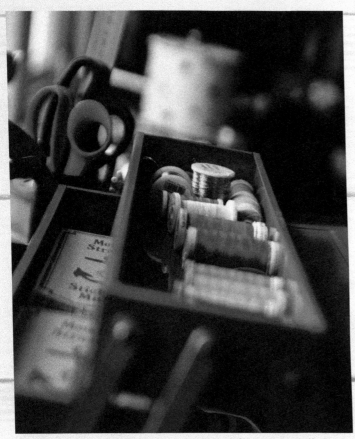

When I moved out of my student house, I was determined to try and find a flat which had access to outside space. The house had a garden, which I took full advantage of whenever I needed to work on props or armour that required sanding or the use of aerosols – the proverbial "well-ventilated area." I knew that working on similar items without a private outdoor area would prove difficult, and I was really fortunate to find a flat which had a small rooftop patio, edged with a series of low stone walls. Again, space is limited, and working out there is not always comfortable, but it means that I don't have to work on the pavement to avoid asphyxiating myself with paint or glue fumes. The low stone walls have also come in handy for riveting – because, let's face it, there's no quiet or delicate way to bang in a rivet!

The one snag when it comes to the patio is that it's over the front door. When doing any sort of DIY or outdoor creative project, the custom is for work to be done at the back of the house, so my working on projects at the front of the house has certainly given my neighbours quite a bit of entertainment. For example: Halloween 2016, a friend of mine who owns a pub commissioned me to make some large props to decorate the place, and one of these was a full-size coffin. I was able to assemble the bulk of the coffin inside, but when it came to decorating I had to take it onto the patio – I'd decided to simulate brass 'studs' on the lid using drawing pins, and needed to hammer them in. I laid the lid, which had been painted black, flat on the stone wall and set to work. Half an hour into it, two older ladies came walking down the street, and naturally looked up to see what I was doing. Their looks of curiosity turned to confusion, then to disbelief when they saw that I was happily hammering into a coffin lid. Seeing as this could rapidly turn awkward, I smiled and called down "It's alright, it's for Halloween!" Much relief from the ladies at this admission, and one called back up that she'd initially thought I was "putting together some roofing, or something terribly practical like that." Thinking back on it, she seemed somewhat disappointed that I was working on something comparatively frivolous. Obviously there's no pleasing some people.

limitation – not to mention my hand-finishing skills have picked up pretty nicely as well!

Secondary to the coffee table is the desk in my bedroom; a nice, sturdy piece of furniture I was able to bring from my parent's house. Originally designed as a dressing table, it doubles as my computer desk and my space for fine detail work on both props and accessories. I have a small cutting mat which sits nicely in front of the keyboard, a selection of brushes and scalpels to one side, and my stock of PVA glue and sealants hides very neatly behind the computer screen. I do a lot of work with papier-mâché – a medium which I feel is often sadly neglected these days – which takes both precision and patience, and I find that the space allows me a lot of natural light to work by throughout the day, as well as being somewhere "safe" where I can leave small, delicate pieces to dry or set without fear of damage.

Equally peculiar was the occasion when I was repainting a male shop mannequin (very muscular and very naked) which had been donated to a museum I volunteer at – during which next door's young family returned from an afternoon out somewhere. I had a very fun chat with the two little girls and their father as to what I was up to, why I had to paint outside, and why I was wearing a face mask and goggles while I was doing it. Still to this day I am grateful that their angle from the pavement looking upwards meant that they could only see the mannequin from the torso upwards! I think it's fair to say that I have acquired something of a reputation on my street.

Whilst I have taught myself the skill of adapting my work to confined spaces, I have also done pretty well in organising what storage space I have to my best advantage. I am fortunate that my bedroom has a built-in cupboard, which I use to keep my collection of footwear and crafting supplies out of harm's way. Under-bed plastic boxes are my friends when it comes to storing fabric; I must have about four of them tucked away under there. Neither do I think there is a single cupboard in the flat that doesn't have something of mine – paints, tools or hats – stored neatly on top of it in a range of attractive boxes. Lastly, but by no means least, are my secret weapons; two ottomans which I inherited from my grandmother, in which I store yet more fabric. They sit beneath the windows in the living room, side by side, and get used as window seats. The only thing I cannot really "hide" is my dressmakers' dummy, but this quite neatly tucks away into a corner of the living room, and most visitors don't even realise that it's there.

So, my advice for creating cosplay in a limited or shared space essentially boils down to one element; planning. This naturally becomes easier the more experienced a cosplayer you become, as you get to grips with whichever making techniques and skills you prefer. Picking a project that's feasible for the space available to you is key. Ambition is commendable, yet it's likely that an attempt to build a 6ft mecha-suit in a second floor bedsit will run into difficulties. Break the construction process into discrete stages, so that should you need to halt a project

or move pieces from one area to another, you can do so without damaging your work. Finally, think of where and how you're going to store it all – both cosplay and crafting supplies – once you've finished. After having put in all that effort into a project, you're going to want to make sure your cosplay stays looking its best for as long as possible, so consider carefully how you're going to condense everything once it's built. Lack of space need not be a limitation; it's a case of discovering how best to make that space work for you.

Alyson Leeds

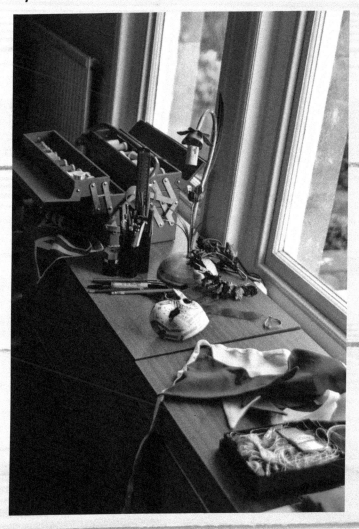

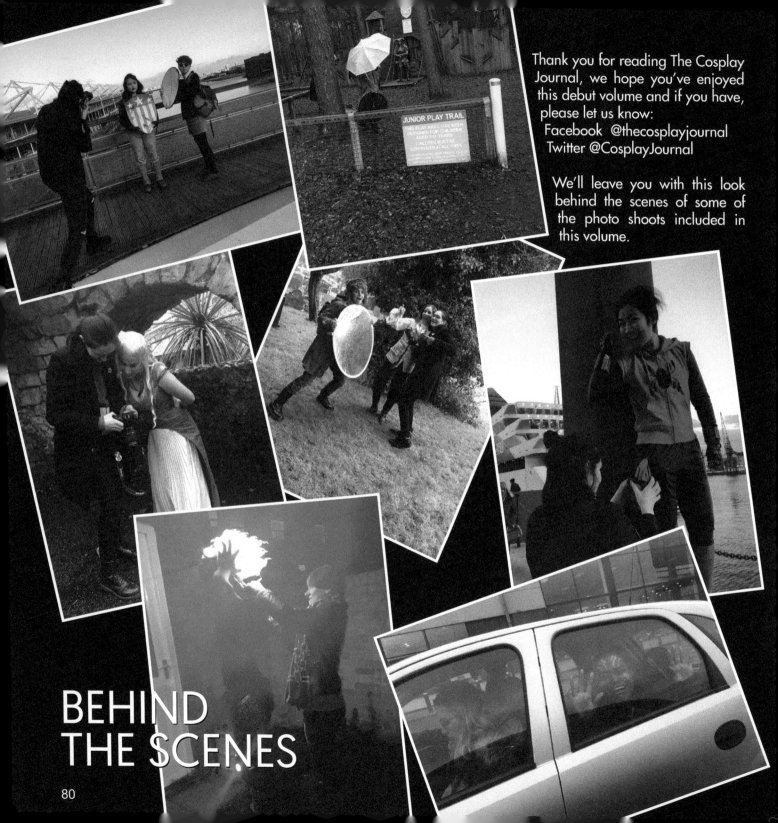

Thank you for reading The Cosplay Journal, we hope you've enjoyed this debut volume and if you have, please let us know:
Facebook @thecosplayjournal
Twitter @CosplayJournal

We'll leave you with this look behind the scenes of some of the photo shoots included in this volume.

BEHIND THE SCENES

Lightning Source UK Ltd.
Milton Keynes UK
UKHW05f1408060618
323805UK00007B/48/P